the power of
kabbalah

Technology for the Soul™

the power of
kabbalah

Technology for the Soul™

Yehuda Berg

www.kabbalah.com™

For further information:

The Kabbalah Centre
155 E. 48th St., New York, NY 10017
1062 S. Robertson Blvd., Los Angeles, CA 90035

1.800.Kabbalah
www.kabbalah.com

4th Edition, May 2004
Printed in USA
ISBN 1-57189-250-8

Design: Hyun Min Lee

In seeking wisdom, the first stage is silence,
the second listening, the third remembrance,
the fourth practicing, the fifth teaching.

— Kabbalist Solomon Gabirol

Dedication

I dedicate this book to my brother, Michael.
May your book, *Becoming Like God*, help everyone become
like God.

Table of Contents

Acknowledgments

I would like to thank the many people who have made this book possible.

First and foremost, Rav and Karen Berg, my parents and teachers. I will be forever thankful for your continual guidance, wisdom, and unconditional support. I am just one of the many whom you have touched with your love and wisdom.

Michael Berg, my brother, for your constant support and friendship, and for your vision and strength. Your presence in my life inspires me to become the best that I can be.

My wife, Michal, for your love and commitment; for your silent power; for your beauty, clarity, and uncomplicated ways. You are the strong foundation that gives me the security to soar.

David, Moshe, Channa, and Yakov, the precious gifts in my life who remind me every day how much there is to be done to ensure that tomorrow will be better than today.

Billy Phillips, one of my closest friends, for your help in making this book possible. The contribution you make to the Kabbalah Centre every day and in so many ways is appreciated far more than you could possibly know.

To Eitan Yardeni, Michael Shane, Linda Friedman, Peter Guzzardi, Ruth Zilberstein, Mitch Sisskind, Hyun Lee, Christian Witkin, and Esther Sibilia, whose contributions made the physical quality, integrity, and accessibility of this book live up to its spiritual beauty and heritage. Thank you for helping me bring to publication this amazing Kabbalistic knowledge passed on to me by my father,

Rav Berg. Your great care will be forever immortalized in its pages.

To my two special friends—you are a true inspiration, and I love you both very much. You know who you are.

Sometimes people who affect you in extraordinary ways come into your life. To my amazing friend—thank you for coming into mine.

To all the Chevre at the Kabbalah Centres worldwide—the evenings we share together in study fuel my passion to bring the power of Kabbalah to the world. You are a part of me and my family no matter where you might be.

The students of The Kabbalah Centre—your desire to learn, to improve your lives, and to share with the world is an inspiration. The positive changes I see in all of you every day make everything I do worthwhile.

introduction

A Fountainhead of Wisdom

Suppose there was an ancient hidden wisdom that revealed and unified the spiritual and physical laws of life . . .

Suppose this wisdom was the true source of all spiritual teachings and religions on this planet, predating Jesus, Muhammad, Moses, Adam and Eve, and even Creation of the world itself . . .

Suppose its insights had a profound influence on the foremost thinkers throughout history, including the abovementioned great souls . . .

Suppose a small circle of eminent sages had long ago grasped this wisdom and recorded it in books that were concealed for two millennia . . .

Finally, suppose this hidden wisdom revealed all the secrets of the universe, all the answers to your questions, all the solutions to your problems.

This wisdom exists, although it's been kept under wraps throughout much of human history.

The wisdom is called Kabbalah, and the visionaries who dared to contemplate and expound upon its mysteries were known as Kabbalists.

The major text of Kabbalah is called the Zohar, and its powerful teachings have influenced the world's most brilliant spiritual, philosophical, religious, and scientific minds—while remaining unknown to humanity at large. (See "A Brief History of Kabbalah" at the end of this book on page 230 for a detailed outline of Kabbalah's dramatic impact upon the world.)

The Secret's Out

The process of bringing this wisdom into the hands of people just like you began some 2,000 years ago with the books of the Zohar, the authoritative body of knowledge on Kabbalah, and their author, a giant among Kabbalists, Rav Shimon bar Yohai. During the centuries that followed, a long line of courageous Kabbalists were maliciously scorned and violently persecuted by the religious establishment for their efforts to make Kabbalah and the teachings of the Zohar available to people from all walks of life. Blood was spilled, and lives were tragically ruined.

Ironically, after their passing, these same Kabbalists were suddenly held in the highest esteem by those who had spurned them. This has been the pattern for over 20 centuries.

You are now able to read this book of long-lost wisdom—thanks, primarily, to three men. They are the true Kabbalists of our era:

Kabbalist Rav Ashlag

Kabbalist Rav Brandwein

Kabbalist Rav Berg

I'm proud to say that Rav Berg happens to be my father, my teacher, my mentor, and my friend. Rav Brandwein was my father's master, and Rav Ashlag was Rav Brandwein's beloved teacher.

The true distinction of these men is their uncommon ability to make lofty and complex teachings intelligible to the layperson. Throughout history, scientists, philosophers, and physicians secretly probed Kabbalah for ideas and notions that eventually helped shape the leading philosophical and scientific doctrines. Scholars explored Kabbalah for intellectual and academic purposes. But while one may be a brilliant scholar of classical music, only a Mozart can compose a symphonic masterpiece.

Rav Berg, Rav Brandwein, and Rav Ashlag are the true virtuosos of Kabbalah, the authentic custodians of this wisdom. Their lineage dates back to Abraham the Patriarch, in a time-honored tradition that preserved the wisdom in its original, uncorrupted form.

Their intent was not a Nobel Prize, academic acclaim, or endless philosophical discourse; the goal of these Kabbalists was to bring simple happiness, permanent peace, and never-ending fulfillment to all humanity.

In the end, is anything more important than that?

Please Be Warned

There remains in effect a single warning, a strict prohibition concerning the wisdom and the lessons of Kabbalah. This warning
dates from the second century, and it is the first of 13 Kabbalistic
Principles of Life that will be presented in this book:

Don't Believe a Word of What You Read!
Belief Won't Cut It!

It has been said that Kabbalah addresses all the age-old questions that have intrigued people throughout time, including these:

- Is there a God?

- Why is life so filled with chaos, pain, and a whole of hurt?

- Why are we here at all?

- How can we achieve uninterrupted fulfillment in our lives?

Some say Kabbalah is not just a light at the end of the tunnel, but
the Light that burns away and removes the tunnel itself, opening
up whole new dimensions of meaning and awareness.

Kabbalah tells us many things: How and why the world began;
why we keep reverting back to our old negative habits; why we
keep avoiding activities we know are good and beneficial to our
lives; why chaos bothers to exist; how to instill meaning and spiritual power into every waking moment.

That's an impressive statement—but don't believe it. Not one
word. Not for one second. The very idea of belief implies a residue

of doubt, but *knowing* leaves no trace of skepticism. It means certainty. Complete conviction. In your gut. In your heart. In your soul.

So, please test each lesson of this book. Apply these principles to your life. Live the lessons, and see if your life gets better. Breathe the lessons, and see if the "air" gets cleaner.

Much sacrifice and suffering has taken place so that in our day a book like this can reach you and the rest of humanity. It is therefore important for all of us to heed the Kabbalistic precept that states, "No coercion in spirituality."

In other words, the intent of this book is not to preach, but rather to humbly teach. For that reason, do not accept these lessons blindly. There must be tangible results in your direct experience. When that happens, you will feel the truth of Kabbalah in your body and soul, and you will come to know the wisdom of the Kabbalistic sages in your heart.

The Language of Simplicity

The Power of Kabbalah is a book that's both lighthearted and profoundly serious. When you read these chapters in the same spirit, you'll find fun and insight at the same time. Wisdom doesn't have to be complex, humdrum, and heavy. In fact, my father taught me something important at a very early age: When striving to understand the mysteries of our universe and the ultimate truths of our existence, how will we know if something is, indeed, truthful? The litmus test is simplicity. Authentic truth is always comprehensible to everyone, even children, and not just to the intellectual elite. If an idea or notion is complex and convoluted, chances are it's not the truth.

A real Kabbalist is one who knows how to make the complicated uncomplicated. That was the true genius of my father's teacher and his teacher's teacher. So don't be fooled by the simplicity and lightheartedness of this book.

In Kabbalah, after all, wisdom is called the *Light!*

Misconceptions about Kabbalah

Those who danced were thought to be quite insane
by those who could not hear the music.
   — Angela Monet

In ancient times, the word Kabbalah struck fear into the hearts of most religious leaders. Shrouded in secrecy and centuries ahead of its time in its speculations, Kabbalah became subject to false rumors and suspicions. Imagine yourself trying to explain the concept of a telephone or the Internet to people of the 15th or 16th centuries. You'd be branded as a mystic, and Kabbalah was called mysticism for the very same reason. But what was once considered mysticism is now called science. As the renowned writer Arthur C. Clarke put it, "Any sufficiently advanced technology is indistinguishable from magic."

Kabbalah was and continues to be the original technology of life. It's the science of the soul and the physics (and metaphysics) of fulfillment. And because it was an innovative wisdom that appeared on the scene thousands of years before its time, it was engulfed in misunderstanding—including the warning that Kabbalah can make you crazy.

That's right! Long ago it was thought that the study of Kabbalah could drive people to madness, to which this book responds . . .

Let's Get Crazy!

If our society defines sanity as heart attacks, panic attacks, ozone cracks, homicide, genocide, suicide, airline crashes, stock market crashes, ethnic clashes, high school shootings, religious feuding, recession, depression, therapy sessions, family welfare, chemical warfare, claustrophobia, xenophobia, unemployment, missile deployments, persecution, executions, political payoffs, massive layoffs, tabloids, steroids, illness, loneliness, earthquakes, poisoned lakes, disease, drug addiction, and death—then yes, Kabbalah can make you crazy!

So, are you ready to get a little bit loony?

Wonderful!

part one
who are we?

The Makeup of Humanity

Who are we? What is our basic makeup? What is our substance, our essence, our core being? What essential element are we made of? Did you ever stop and truly contemplate that question? Kabbalah defines us in one simple word:

Desire!

Desire in Motion

When Kabbalah uses the word *desire* to define us, it is not a metaphor. Desire is truly our essential quality. Desire is the stuff we're made of. It is our essence. Desire is what drives us. It's what makes us tick. We are all desires on foot, constantly seeking to fulfill our own cravings. Our hearts beat, our blood flows, our bodies move, solely because there's a desire and urge seeking to be fulfilled. Kabbalist Rav Ashlag once wrote that humans would not twitch a single finger if not for some inner desire.

Desire and Diversity

At heart, our individual human desires give us our separate identities.

Some people desire sexual fulfillment. Some desire intellectual fulfillment. Some want religious fulfillment. Others seek the material kind. Some of us desire fame. Others seek solitude. Some seek enlightenment. Some of us seek travel and adventure. Many look to riches and wealth to satiate their appetite for life. And there are those who seek academic assets to quench their thirst.

According to Kabbalah, human desires basically operate on three levels:

Level One

These desires are rooted in animal lust. A person's needs, wants, and learned behaviors exist only to gratify these primal urges. The desire to eat, the urge to sleep, the craving for sex (not love) are all Level One desires. People at Level One may make use of rational, intellectual thought, as all human beings do, but it is for the purpose of serving their animal desire. "A slave is never more than its master," states Kabbalist Rav Ashlag.

Level Two

These desires are directed toward fulfilling drives not found in the animal kingdom, such as honor, power, prestige, fame, and dominion over others. The needs, and consequently the thoughts, conscious choices, decisions, and actions, of people at Level Two are directed only toward gratifying these desires to the fullest extent.

Level Three

The desires of this level are directed mainly toward rational matters. They are oriented toward gratifying an intellectually driven desire to its fullest. This includes the yearning for wisdom, knowledge, and answers.

"These three types of desire," Rav Ashlag states, "are found in all members of the human race; however, they are blended in each individual in different proportions, and it is this that makes for the differences that exist between one man and another."

A Vessel

In the language of Kabbalah, desire is referred to as a *Vessel*. A Vessel is like an empty cup that seeks to be filled. Unlike an empty physical cup, however, the Vessel of our desires is not founded upon anything material. For instance, remember the time you consumed a sizzling steak to the point of nearly bursting the buttons on your shirt? You couldn't eat another morsel. But then the dessert cart was wheeled over to your table and you found yourself staring at a tray of seductive sweets. Although your stomach was full, your new desire for something sweet managed to make a little room, and the next thing you knew, you were gobbling up Black Forest cake. Although there may eventually be a limit to your appetite, there is no limit to your desire.

Every activity in this world is founded upon some inner urge, large or small, yearning to be fulfilled. It's as though we have no free will in the matter. We live life on autopilot, driven by the constant need to nourish all the longings that linger in both our body and soul.

The Object of Our Desire

So, what do our hearts truly desire? It would be safe to say that the primary objective of our desire is uninterrupted happiness, although *happiness* may mean something different to each person.

In fact, desiring continual happiness is the one unifying link of all humanity. You don't have to convince a criminal, a lawyer, a construction worker, a CEO, a wicked person, a kind person, an atheist, a pious person, a mogul, or a pauper to want constant happiness. The desire for endless happiness is our very essence.

A scientist might desire truth and an understanding of the laws that govern our physical world. On another level, a scientist may also desire a Nobel Prize and a permanent place in history. Perhaps a politician desires to improve his or her community, city, state, or country. Or maybe the politician is looking for personal privileges, influence, and prominence. A child generally desires play and pleasure. A stand-up comic might desire laughter, love, fame, and acceptance. A CEO usually desires financial achievement and power. A factory worker probably desires a vacation, food on the table, and peace of mind. Scholars generally desire knowledge and academic acclaim from their peers.

However you define them, all the objects of our desires are really just different packages of fulfillment. These various containers of contentment set us in motion and shape our lives.

Kabbalah sums up all these different packages of fulfillment into one word . . .

Light!

The Power of Light

The term *Light* is merely a code word, a metaphor offered by the ancient Kabbalists to convey the broad spectrum of fulfillment for which human beings long.

Did you ever gaze at a beam of sunlight after a cool rain on a hot summer day? When the shaft of sunlight strikes a droplet of water in the air, the light refracts into the seven colors of the rainbow. Think about that image. Just as this single ray of white sunlight includes all the colors of the spectrum, the word *Light* suggests all the "colors" of joy that people seek in their lives.

There is one distinct difference, however, between the metaphor of sunlight and the Light described by Kabbalah. The white light of the sun includes a mere seven colors in its spectrum. The Light that Kabbalah speaks of contains an infinite amount of "colors." In other words, every conceivable form of fulfillment and pleasure that a soul can yearn for is contained within the Light. This includes the joy of sex and the ecstasy of chocolate. It also includes the force of healing, the power of prosperity, and the bliss of a loving, passionate relationship.

Light also consists of the force that we call intuition. The magic that attracts the right people and right opportunities to our lives. The force that activates our immune systems. The inner spirit that arouses hope and optimism within us each morning we wake. The fuel that generates our self-motivation to seek more and more out of life.

The Light Stays On

But Light is not defined solely as happiness and joy. Kabbalistically, Light denotes *unending* happiness, constant joy. It's the difference between momentary pleasure and lasting fulfillment. We don't really want a short-lived, pleasurable high. Our deepest desires are not limited to 15 minutes of fame. Or a temporary rush from closing a killer business deal. Or a quick-fix high from drugs. Or temporary relief from a painkiller. We don't want to be liked and adored by our friends and colleagues for just a limited period of time. We don't want to be healthy for just half of our lives. We don't want passionate sexual relations with our spouses for just the first two months of a 25 year-relationship. We want our desires to be constantly filled. This constant, continuous, nonstop flow of fulfillment is what Kabbalah defines as Light.

The Root of Our Unhappiness

The fact that our desires are not constantly infused with Light is the foundation of our unhappiness and anxiety. If we had joy in an area of our lives for five years, it means there was only enough Light in the "tank" to last for those five years. Running out of Light—or rather, disconnecting from Light—made us unhappy. The more Light we have in our lives, the longer our desires remain fulfilled and the happier we are.

We also have a lingering deep-seated fear that our happiness will eventually end. When we find ourselves in a rare state of contentment and serenity, we have a negative tendency to believe it's too good to be true. We worry about tomorrow. And the moment these doubts creep in, the instant we begin to worry about how long our happiness will last, we run out of Light. We lose the connection. Light is therefore also defined as the comfort, security, and peace of mind of knowing that happiness will still be with us tomorrow. When we are connected to the Light, we have no fear, anxiety, or insecurity about the future.

Ultimate Desire

In light of the above (pun intended!), the Kabbalists tell us that a human being's ultimate desire is desire for Light. Moreover, the Kabbalists tell us that this Light is everywhere. It is the most common substance in our universe. It fills the cosmos and saturates our reality. This Light is infinite. Boundless. And always ready to fulfill more than we can imagine. Which leads us to a compelling question:

If people are the essence of desire,
and the universe is flooded with Light,
what stands in the way of our
everlasting happiness?

ANSWER: A curtain.

Two Sides of the Curtain: The 1 Percent and the 99 Percent

According to Kabbalah, there is a curtain that divides our reality into two realms, which Kabbalah identifies as the 1 percent and the 99 percent. The 1 percent realm encompasses our physical world. But this is only a tiny fraction of all Creation. It is only what we perceive with our five senses—what we can smell, taste, touch, see, and hear. And that is a mere fragment of what is truly "out there."

On the other side of the curtain lies the 99 percent, which encompasses the vast majority of reality.

In the 1 percent realm, life has an annoying habit of catching us off guard. We are afflicted with something called the Suddenly Syndrome:

He had a sudden heart attack.
All of a sudden, he walked out on her.
Suddenly, we're short of cash.
The deal suddenly fell through.
She suddenly changed her mind.
The doctors suddenly found a lump.
Life suddenly felt so empty.

But is there really such a thing as "suddenly"? Kabbalah says no. Absolutely not. There is always a concealed, unseen cause that precedes any "sudden" event.

Did you ever wake up one morning to suddenly find a full-grown oak tree standing tall on your front lawn? Of course not. Somewhere in the past a seed was planted. When a nasty problem suddenly pops up and cuts off the flow of happiness that was fulfilling a particular desire of yours, according to Kabbalah this is not just some random, chaotic event. There exists a deeper cause. Somewhere in the past, a seed was planted. The biggest mistake we make in life is believing that there are mistakes or accidental circumstances. There are no mistakes. There are no coincidences. No accidents. And no sudden catastrophes. Whatever happens, happens for a reason.

Chaos Theory

The Suddenly Syndrome originates in our inability to see through the illusions of our lives in the 1 percent realm. We cannot see beyond the immediate turmoil in order to grasp the big picture. We cannot see the other side of the curtain where the larger reality resides. Meteorologists faced this same problem when trying to predict weather. Storms and other fluctuations in the atmospheric conditions occurred without warning. They concluded that weather was a chaotic, nonlinear, and random sequence of events. Further scientific study, however, revealed a mysterious order concealed within the chaos. Science calls this phenomenon the butterfly effect.

The Butterfly Effect

Incredible as it seems, scientists discovered that the tiny turbulence created by a butterfly flapping its wings in Tokyo can eventually amplify into a tornado in Kansas. And a person slamming a car door in Iowa can therefore influence the weather in Brazil. Everything is connected on a deeper level of reality. Weather only appears random to meteorologists because they are unable to perceive and measure all the millions of influences that contribute to a stormy day—such as flapping butterflies and slamming doors.

Kabbalah revealed this concept centuries ago. Our lives, no matter how chaotic they may appear, contain order hiding within. The problem is that a curtain limits our ability to spot all those tiny butterflies blowing the winds of chaos into our personal lives. Nevertheless, all the storms and tornadoes whipping through our daily existence have their own unseen causes hiding behind the curtain. We observe effects but not the cause level of reality. We experience symptoms but are oblivious to their underlying root. We undergo chaos but cannot detect its origin. We are blind to the remaining 99 percent.

So, here we are, in touch with a microscopic portion of reality as we desperately search it for fulfillment of our deepest desires. Some of us turn to science, some to traditional religion, some to drugs. Some pursue wealth and power. But the inner void remains. We feel insignificant, helpless, unhappy, and out of control, starving for spiritual sustenance, meaning, and positive change.

Will we remain prisoners of this 1 percent realm and miss out on 99 percent of reality? Will we be doomed to chaos and darkness?

Must the curtain remain up forever?

Not by a long shot.

The 99 Percent World

A physicist had a horseshoe hanging on the door of his laboratory. His colleagues were surprised and asked whether he believed that it would bring luck to his experiments. He answered, "No, I don't believe in superstitions. But I have been told that it works even if you don't believe in it."
— R. L. Weber, *A Random Walk in Science*

The familiar reality is the 1 percent world in which we live, yet there is another side to this curtain—the 99 percent—and it is ultimately far more important. According to Kabbalah, the 99 percent realm is the source of all lasting fulfillment. All knowledge, wisdom, and joy dwell in this realm. This is the domain the Kabbalists call Light. Whenever we experience joy, we've made contact with this realm through some action that has taken place in the 1 percent realm. It might be from the hug of your child. Or perhaps you just closed a significant business deal. But the joy you feel flows from the 99 percent.

Nothing New Under the Sun

Before Thomas Edison, civilization lived pretty much in the dark compared to the 24-hour, neon-lit, fluorescent-glowing, halogen-burning world of today. But did Edison really invent something new when he produced the first light bulb? Or did the information on how to build a light bulb already exist?

In other words, if someone had had the same information and materials for building a light bulb 100 years before Edison, couldn't the light have been switched on much sooner?

Did Albert Einstein actually discover something new with his Theory of Relativity, or was it always there?

Did Isaac Newton invent gravity when he discovered its properties, or did gravity always exist?

Edison, Einstein, and Newton merely revealed something that already existed. So, where was all this information hiding before these great minds uncovered it? The answer, according to Kabbalah, is behind the curtain, in the 99 percent world.

Timeless Symphony

Mozart said he was able to conceive entire symphonies in his mind before he wrote a single note. When he mentally experienced an hour of music in just a split second, Mozart felt that he was tapping into another reality. He was transcending the laws of time and space, and entering a spiritual dimension. This other reality that Mozart tapped into is the 99 percent.

Similarly, great scientific minds of the past believed that spiritual insight played a role in their achievements. Today, scientists are beginning to recognize that the spiritual dimension can be a source of great insight and inspiration.

Consider the case of Russian chemist Dmitry Mendeleyev, who had an unusual dream in 1869. Said Mendeleyev:

I saw in a dream a table where all the elements fell into place as required. Awakening, I immediately wrote it down on a piece of paper.

Mendeleyev's dream resulted in the periodic table of the elements we all learned about in our high school chemistry classes.

Insulin, used to treat diabetics, was discovered by Canadian physician Sir Frederick Banting. Banting had a dream that hinted at a method for extracting the substance from a nonhuman pancreas. Banting won the Nobel Prize and was eventually knighted for his discoveries.

American inventor Elias Howe dreamed about being chased by cannibals with spears. While the natives were waving their weapons, he noticed that the shafts all had tiny holes in them. The spears were also bobbing up and down. After this dream, Howe was finally able to complete his invention of the automatic sewing machine. He realized that he had to move the eye of the needle to the bottom of the needle instead of placing it at the top.

Renowned scientist Niels Bohr claimed that he dreamed of sitting on the sun with all the planets hissing around on tiny cords. Thereafter, Bohr developed the model of the atom.

Robert Louis Stevenson reported that the theme for his classic story, Dr. Jekyll and Mr. Hyde, originated in a dream, as did much of his best work.

The great Greek philosopher Plato spoke about the Platonic realm, a world of ideas, which he said was the origin and true source of our physical reality and all wisdom. Our world was merely a shadow of this hidden reality.

In his book, Shadows of the Mind, eminent physicist Roger Penrose wrote:

> According to Plato, mathematical concepts and mathe-
> matical truths inhabit an actual world of their own that is
> timeless and without physical location. Plato's world is an
> ideal world of perfect forms, distinct from the physical
> world, but in terms of which the physical world must be
> understood.

Guess where Plato derived this compelling idea? According to most of the great minds of the scientific revolution, including the philosophers Henry More and Wilhelm Leibniz, Plato liberated this idea from the ancient Kabbalah!

The Moment of Connection

Plato called a connection to the 99 percent "divine madness."

Famed philosopher Nicholas of Cusa called it "divine revelation" or *docta ignorantia.*

Mozart described it as "a rush."

Philosopher Edmund Husserl called it "pure intuition" and "intuition."

Our moms called it "a mother's intuition."

Your Aunt Rose termed it her "sixth sense."

Successful businesspeople call it a "gut instinct."

A Brief Summary of the 1 Percent

The 1 percent reality is the world of our five senses. It is a realm of spiritual darkness and chaos in which:

We react to external events

Fulfillment is temporary and happiness is fleeting

Effects, symptoms, and reactions preoccupy us

We are victims who apparently suffer because of other people's actions and random external circumstances

There seems to be no hope for bringing about permanent, positive change because any change that occurs is temporary and therefore illusory

The majority of our desires remain unfulfilled

Murphy's Law governs the realm of the 1 percent. Everything that can possibly go wrong will go wrong. Even when things go well, we know they'll change, for we live in an endless cycle of up and down, lucky and unlucky.

When we live our lives solely in the 1 percent, life hurts and the world appears dark and disordered.

A Brief Summary of the 99 Percent

The 99 percent reality lies beyond human perception. It is:

A world of absolute order, perfection, and infinite spiritual Light

A realm of action rather than reaction to external events

The source, the seed, and the hidden origin of the physical world

A world of total fulfillment, infinite knowledge, and endless joy

A dimension in which we can initiate positive, lasting change, permanent change that also manifests in our 1 percent world

There is no trace of Murphy's Law in the realm of the 99 percent. When we live our lives connecting to the 99 percent level, life is fulfilling, energy flows, and the world appears bright and beautiful.

This leads us to our Second Kabbalistic Principle:

Two Basic Realities Exist:
Our 1 Percent World of Darkness
and the 99 Percent Realm of Light!

20th-Century Science Stumbles Upon the 99 Percent

Dr. Stuart Hameroff is a doctor of medicine, a professor of anesthesiology and psychology, and the associate director of the Center for Consciousness Studies at the University of Arizona. Professor Hameroff, along with renowned Oxford physicist Sir Roger Penrose, has been researching the nature of human consciousness.

Dr. Hameroff was intrigued by the ancient Kabbalist's description of the 99 percent realm and its similarity to the quantum mechanical view of our universe.

Hameroff states:

> For 100 years it has been known that there exists two worlds, the classical world we experience with our five senses and the quantum world. We live in the classical world where everything seems "normal" (if unfulfilling). Everything has a definite shape, place and substance. However, at very small scales the quantum world reigns and everything is strange and bizarre, defying common sense.

> Science knows very little about the quantum world, but we now believe that the quantum world is a vast storage house of information including Platonic values such as good versus evil, beauty, truth and wisdom. To me, these are indications that the quantum world qualifies as the 99 percent reality that Kabbalah speaks of, and that a curtain does indeed exist between the two worlds.

So, we now have the ancient Kabbalist, the modern-day scientist, and the most famous philosopher of history (Plato) telling us that the 99 percent, though undetected by the five senses, is a far more real and authentic reality than our entire physical world. It sure took long enough to get consensus on the nature of reality.

The Problem

There is one nagging obstacle—it's our inability to control the moments of connection to the 99 percent realm. Accessing this dimension of Light is accidental and haphazard at best. Looking at it from the perspective of the big picture, it seems that only a few great minds in every generation were able to connect to the 99 percent to uncover a piece of wisdom that drastically altered the destiny of humanity. Once again, think of Einstein, Newton, Mozart, Moses, Muhammad, Jesus, and Abraham.

On a personal level, prior to our reading this book, most of us probably never even knew that such a blissful realm of existence even existed. Consequently, when we did make contact with the 99 percent—our past moments of intuition, creative inspiration, meeting the right people, experiencing a miracle, formulating brilliant ideas etc.,—we thought it was just good old fashioned lady luck shining down upon us. It's difficult for us to recognize something we cannot see or touch.

My father, Kabbalist Rav Berg, describes the 99 percent reality as dancing on the edge of consciousness, like an enchanting dream that cannot quite be remembered. Moments before waking, there is a crucial instant when only a loose thread connects the dreamer to the dream. The harder the dreamer pulls on that delicate strand, the more quickly the fabric of the dream unravels and disappears. As the dreamer tries to reattach the thread, the dream fades and the dreamer must become resolved to a waking reality immensely inferior to that of the dream.

Imagine if we could access this realm at will; we would gain the ability to control all the events in our lives. Instead of dealing with symptoms and effects, we could discover the hidden forces behind chaotic circumstances and maddening events that "suddenly" end our happiness, leaving our deepest desires unfulfilled. We would have the power to create order out of chaos. We could utilize the Light of the 99 percent to vanish any form of darkness in our lives. According to Kabbalah, this is the only way to effect genuine change.

Think of it this way: If you alter a branch of a tree, you change the branch. Modify a leaf, and you change the leaf. But if you can manipulate the genetic information inside the seed, you can affect the entire tree—branches, leaves, fruit, the whole shebang.

The realm of the 99 percent is the DNA level of reality: The seed. The root. The cause of all causes.

Chasing Our Own Shadows

Consider the following analogy. Your shadow on a sidewalk presents a severely limited version of your true self. Your shadow does not reflect the skin, hair, blood, bones, emotions, imagination, feelings, or desires that define you as an individual. It is merely a two-dimensional reflection of your three-dimensional reality, a 1 percent picture of your true 99 percent self. In this example, the shadow corresponds to the 1 percent world. Your true self corresponds to the dimension that lies beyond the five senses—that is, to the 99 percent.

Could you move someone's arm simply by touching his or her shadow on the wall? It can't be done. You must touch the source, the actual arm, the 99 percent. You must move into a higher dimension to effect change: Move the actual arm, and the shadow responds automatically!

But we've been conditioned to focus our awareness on the 1 percent realm of existence, which is akin to chasing our own shadows. Kabbalah says that won't cut it. It's an exercise in futility.

Here's a simple experiment you can try at home, right now, that should solidify the point:. Get a piece of paper and a pencil, then write down your top five responses to the following question:

What does a human being truly desire from life?

The Top Ten List

When this question was asked to tens of thousands of people learning Kabbalah over the years, the following items turned up most frequently:

- Personal fulfillment

- Peace of mind

- Relief from fear and anxiety

- Financial security

- Contentment

- Love

- Freedom

- Control

- Wisdom

- Happiness

- Health

Chances are, your list has something in common with this top ten list. Notice that not one of these items can be measured or weighed on a scale or held in your hands. You cannot physically locate any of these items on a map or reach them by geographically defining their coordinates. None of the things that we most want to receive from life is of a physical nature. Nothing on our list is found in the material 1 percent realm—even financial security (which is a feeling). Everything we genuinely desire is of an ethereal nature found only in the 99 percent reality.

Thus, our Third Kabbalistic Principle states:

**Everything That a Human Being
Truly Desires from Life
Is Spiritual Light!**

So, what do we do throughout our lives? We chase physical possessions in our pursuit of happiness!

To see how this principle operates, let's look at something that would seem to be a very tangible asset: money. Cold, hard cash. Consider an individual with a net worth of $20 million who loses $15 million overnight in a stock market crash. Compare that to a person with a net worth of $20,000 who suddenly earns $80,000 from a stock that just went through the roof. Which one goes to bed with greater financial peace of mind and a stronger sense of security? The one who still has $5 million, or the one with only a small fraction of that amount?

According to Kabbalah, material objects are not what we're really seeking in life. We're really searching for the spiritual energy that pervades the 99 percent world.

The Reason for Our Discontent

We find ourselves unhappy, unfulfilled, sad, depressed, miserable, or anxious when our desires seem to be ignored by the universe. It's usually some form of chaos that precipitates our unfulfilled longings. Ill health. Financial adversity. Problems in the marriage. Social pressures. Fears, phobias, and panic attacks. All this turmoil occurs for one reason and one reason only:

We have disconnected ourselves, knowingly or unknowingly, from the 99 percent realm.

However, when we learn how to connect to this realm, we can control the events in our lives. We can prevent and eradicate the chaos that causes our unhappiness. We can turn on the Light and vanquish the darkness.

Contact with the 99 percent realm is the secret key to fulfillment in life. But it's not easy to do. That's why the ancient masters of Kabbalah gave us the tools and methods for reaching beyond our everyday lives. In the pages that follow, we'll explore and explain these tools in great detail.

It Makes You Wonder . . .

Why do chaos, suffering, pain, and disease exist if there is another world of order and happiness?

Why are there even such things as 1 percent and 99 percent realms?

Who constructed reality in that way? And for what reason?

Why is it that other spiritual systems teach us wisdom, but life still never really changes?

Why are our desires and the fulfillment we seek separated by some unseen curtain?

Who hung up the curtain?

How do we inadvertently disconnect ourselves from the 99 percent realm?

Where do our desires spring from?

The Taste of Time

A tribesman of the rain forest will not suddenly wake up tomorrow morning and crave a double cappuccino or a double-cheese pizza. Desires do not spring up on their own volition; the taste must have been tasted before. You cannot have a passion to enjoy another viewing of *The Godfather* for the umpteenth time if you never knew of or experienced the film before.

A heroin addict will go to almost any lengths to score another hit. An alcoholic will stop at almost nothing when the craving for a drink appears. The basis for these incessant drives is that the experience of drugs or alcohol is already in the blood. Moreover, people with addictions know that this urge can be fulfilled and the "high" can be reexperienced.

Given that desire springs from experience and memory, isn't it interesting that since the dawn of humanity, people have been unrelenting in their quest for eternal happiness? No matter how many wars, diseases, famines, depressions, and natural disasters knock us off our feet, we keep picking ourselves back up again, ever determined in our quest for lasting comfort, unending joy, and permanent pleasure.

It stands to reason that we must have experienced this 99 percent realm before. Somewhere in the recesses of our souls, we *know* it's possible to connect ourselves to this reality on a continuing basis.

Memories

According to Kabbalah, the very stuff of which the human body is composed—the atoms in our blood, the electrons that spur the impulses in our brains, the chemicals that make up our tissues and our bones—have roots that extend far back before the origin of our physical universe. The various desires, urges, impulses, and cravings that pervade our minds have existed since before the dawn of time. Whatever longings are stirring in our hearts at this very moment are in fact memories lingering in our souls, recollections ingrained into our very being.

The pursuit of happiness is not only inscribed into the Constitution as an inalienable right of U.S. citizenship, it is also present in the blueprint of our universe. It is the inherited birthright of humanity.

Remember: An old oak tree didn't just spring up accidentally on your front lawn out of nowhere. There was a hidden seed. Similarly, there is a seed of our desires and of the fulfillment we so desperately seek.

We will now identify this ancient seed, and discover the ultimate purpose of our "sudden" appearance on the front lawns of this world.

part two
creation, the big bang, and the nature of god

The Cause of All Causes

Know that before the emanations were emanated and the created were created, the exalted and simple Light filled the entire existence, and there was no empty space whatsoever.
— Kabbalist Isaac Luria, 16th century

For countless centuries, questions surrounding the origins of the cosmos were contemplated by rabbis, priests, scientists, shamans, spiritualists, philosophers, and physicists. Today, the scientific establishment largely agrees that some 15 billion years ago, the physical universe exploded into existence in what is now called the Big Bang. But science stops right there, leaving the ultimate question dangling in the vacuum of space:

Why did the Big Bang occur in the first place?

What caused it? And how does the Big Bang relate to life in the big city today? Why should we concern ourselves with something that took place 15 billion years ago when we can't even figure out what went wrong in our life 15 minutes ago?

Only the ancient Kabbalists dared to answer these fundamental questions of existence in practical, down-to-earth terms. They traveled to a place where no one else had ever ventured—to that mysterious moment before the Creation of our universe!

However, before we travel back in time to discover the greatest secrets known to humanity, there is something you first need to know about the secrets themselves.

Wisdom as Light

The Kabbalistic wisdom and concepts that will be revealed in the pages that follow are older than time itself. These are the secrets of all secrets concerning the origin of our souls. These are the mysteries of all mysteries. The benefit attached to learning about our origins extends beyond greater intellectual knowledge. There is a mystical dimension attached to understanding the root of our existence. There is a spiritual benefit that comes with grasping these pristine principles. This long-hidden wisdom, according to the most learned Kabbalists, is also the substance of spiritual Light itself. Each new notion planted in our minds opens up pathways and portals into the 99 percent through which positive energy fills our beings. Learning Kabbalah unleashes hidden potential, allowing us to see and perceive things we never saw before. When you grasp a new principle or idea, or internalize a new piece of wisdom from these pages, another candle is lit and it shines in your soul. That means life gets a little bit better and a little bit brighter. Yes, it is that simple.

The most brilliant minds in history, including Pythagoras, Plato, Newton, and Leibniz, explored Kabbalah's hidden wisdom, and it influenced them in profound ways. The goal in studying Kabbalah and the mysteries of our origins is not just to become more knowledgeable, but also purer, more enlightened, and more fulfilled.

Please do not expect or accept anything less.

Pulling Back the Curtain

Today, with the acceptance of quantum mechanics, relativity, and other leading-edge scientific theories, it appears that science is at last catching up to Kabbalah. As we'll discover in the pages that follow, these scientific viewpoints bear striking similarities to the cosmological speculations of the ancient Kabbalists. One distinct difference remains, however: Whereas science limits its explorations to how the world works, Kabbalah asks the ultimate question, Why?

Why does the world exist as it does?

Why are we here?

Why is my life the way it is?

If you've ever stopped to ask yourself these questions when life presented you with difficult challenges, you have your reason why you should read this chapter.

We're now going to sneak a peek behind the curtain and discover what really lies on the other side of reality. Ready to take a look? Here goes:

Before planet Earth . . .

Before the universe . . .

Before the Big Bang . . .

Back to the cause of all causes . . .

Once upon a time, before there was even a concept such as time, there was only one simple reality . . .

Energy.

Energy

Yes—"before" time even began, there was an infinite force of Energy. This force reached as far as forever. It filled eternity. It expanded into infinity. There were no concepts such as time, space, or motion because, according to Kabbalah, this boundless Energy was the only reality. There was nothing else. Nothing. Just a pure, endless, all-pervading force of stillness.

The Nature of This Force

The Energy had one nature, a single will, which was to:

Share endlessly,

Impart continuously.

Give ceaselessly.

Bestow eternally.

Which begs the question: *Share what?*

The answer: *Itself!*

Namely, the nature of this Energy was to *share Its very essence.*

What the Force Is Made Of

The essence and substance of this Energy was infinite fulfillment, boundless joy, and limitless enlightenment. The Energy is made of all possible forms of pleasure.

Everything we've ever desired, and much more, is included within it:

- Personal fulfillment

- Peace of mind

- Relief from fear and anxiety

- Financial security

- Contentment

- Love

- Freedom

- Control

- Wisdom

- Happiness

- Health

Everything positive that goes against the force of chaos; whatever is the antithesis of suffering and pain; anything that generates fulfillment, pleasure, and passion . . . all of it was included within this boundless force of Energy. This is precisely what the Energy wanted to share and impart.

In Kabbalah, this ever-expanding Energy of giving is also known as the First Cause.

Two to Tango

The concept of giving and sharing requires two consenting parties. After all, if there's no one to share with, how can sharing happen? If there is no one willing to receive the gift, how can the gift be given?

Imagine an old lady on the corner of a busy intersection. A passerby attempts to help her cross the street safely. She politely refuses. He tries again. She still refuses, now somewhat annoyed at his insistence. Why is she annoyed? Because she has no desire to cross the street. She's merely standing at the intersection waiting for the bus to arrive.

Although our passerby wanted to give, giving was impossible because the lady didn't have a desire to receive what he offered. Contemplate this last idea for an extra moment. *There must be a recipient, a willing receiver, an actual desire to take possession of the offering, for sharing or giving to take place.*

The Vessel

To fulfill its giving nature, the infinite force of Energy created a receiver—in Kabbalah it's called a Vessel—with which to share its essence. Imagine a cup full of water. The water inside the cup corresponds to the Energy. The cup corresponds to the Vessel that receives and contains the Energy. The Vessel, however, was not a physical entity. Rather, it was a force, an intelligent, nonmaterial essence.

The nature of the Vessel was an infinite *Desire to Receive*. In other words, for every kind of fulfillment and joy the Energy radiated forth, there was a corresponding Desire to Receive by the Vessel.

Because this Energy force embodied an infinite variety of fulfillment, the Vessel consisted of infinite Desires to Receive.

In down-to-earth terms, if there was sexual energy radiating from this Energy force, then a lustful desire for sex was aroused in the Vessel. If a box of chocolates was included within this Energy, then a sweet tooth and a craving for chocolate were actualized within the Vessel. If a billion dollars' worth of gold bullion was part of the Light, then a desire for enormous wealth was awakened within the Vessel.

Seeing that this Energy force is defined as the First Cause, the Vessel is appropriately defined as the First Effect.

So, we now have an infinite Energy and an infinite Vessel. Cause and effect. Sharing and receiving. Utter perfection. Bliss, beyond human comprehension.

God and Humanity

Let's return to our reality for just a moment. You've probably figured out by now that the Vessel is our root, our seed, our origin, our source. In fact, all the souls of humanity, past and present, were present within the Vessel. Just as one human body is comprised of trillions of cells, the Vessel was comprised of trillions of souls. You and I were like the individual cells of the Vessel.

Throughout the ages, the infinite force of Energy has been called God, Master of the Universe, Divine Creator, and many other names. The ancient Kabbalists referred to this Energy force by the term *the Light*. Why *the Light*?

- As sunlight instantly expands and illuminates a darkened room on this side of the curtain, the Light expands and illuminates eternity on the other side of the curtain.

- As a single ray of light contains all the colors of the rainbow, the Light contains all the colors of fulfillment.

This Light that shines so brightly behind the curtain is the source and substance of all the fulfillment we seek. All of our activities are, in actuality, pursuit of the Light, which manifests in myriad ways: rewarding relationships, prosperous careers, personal accomplishments, rich family life, emotional contentment, financial security, creativity, knowledge, wisdom, and all other goals as we strive for happiness.

This Light is what shines and illuminates the 99 percent.

The Light

The Light is not God, but an Energy that comes from God. Consider sunlight. The photons that fall on the earth are not the source and essence of the fiery solar body that gives us life from a distance of 93 million miles. Similarly, the Light is not actually the Creator, but rather His positive attributes and spiritual energy that radiate from His core. In even simpler terms, just as we cannot touch the nuclear furnace that is our sun, the human mind cannot conceive of the totality of God. It makes little sense, therefore, to ponder the source of infinity when we cannot truly grasp or behold the concept of infinity itself. It's enough to know that the Light's joy and infinite fulfillment will completely and absolutely satisfy any and all human desires.

The Structure of the Vessel

The infinite Vessel was composed of two aspects—a male and a female energy, like a single battery containing positive and negative poles.

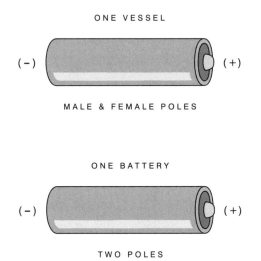

ONE VESSEL

(−)   (+)

MALE & FEMALE POLES

ONE BATTERY

(−)   (+)

TWO POLES

Adam and Eve

Kabbalah teaches that these two energies in one Vessel are known by the code name *Adam and Eve*. You've probably heard of them. Adam and Eve were not just two people in the Garden of Eden. (Some 2,000 years ago, the master Kabbalist Rav Shimon bar Yohai said that whoever takes the Bible literally is a fool—his words, not mine.) The phrase *Adam and Eve* refers to the male-female polarity of the one unified Vessel.

ONE VESSEL

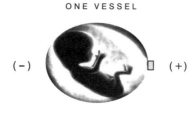

(–)   (+)

MALE & FEMALE POLES

It's a Code!

Kabbalists understand that the entire Bible is a code. And like any complex code, it requires deciphering and deeper understanding. In a sense, it's like music. Imagine trying to feel a composer's emotions simply by looking at sheet music. Unless you're a brilliant musician yourself, it just won't work. You must hear the melody and listen to the performance to fully appreciate the song. Otherwise, you'll never know if you're looking at a sad song or a joyful melody. Kabbalah is the instrument of our universe playing out the song of Creation. The Bible is the sheet music.

Science relies on similar ideas. A physicist would never depend on the appearance of a rock to learn the fundamental nature of its reality at the level of atoms, protons, electrons, and neutrons.

The Bible *also* has a subatomic level far beneath the surface level of the literal text. In fact, the principal reason for the hostility between science and religion, and why religion has failed to fulfill the desires of all people and bring permanent peace to our planet, is that we've been reading the Bible literally. We've remained in the Stone Age concerning its subatomic level. This subatomic level is called Kabbalah. On this level we learn that the code term *Adam and Eve* actually pertains to the one Vessel—which is itself an infinite conscious force known as the Desire to Receive.

One Act of Creation

The creation of the Vessel—that is, the Desire to Receive—is the only true Creation that has ever occurred. That's it. No other entities were constructed. No other worlds were fabricated from scratch. The only thing that ever came into existence—ex nihilo—was the Desire to Receive all that the Light was offering.

This single act of Creation occurred *before* the origin of our universe. Within this one act of Creation, however, there exist countless complex phases, which the ancient Kabbalistic texts have made known through discourse, metaphor, parable, and other cryptic language. Study of these phases requires many years, so an abbreviated rendition will be presented here.

The Light's sharing of its essence with the Vessel led to a remarkable unity. In Kabbalistic terms, this profound unity is called . . .

The Endless World

If we could actually perceive the Endless World while peeking behind the curtain, it would be impossible to distinguish between the Light and the Vessel.

Imagine carving a cup from a block of ice. Then imagine pouring water into this cup. The cup is the receiver—the Vessel. The water is the giver—the Light. Water fills the cup just as the Light fills the Vessel. At their very essence, however, both the water and the cup are H_2O. One essence, but two forms. The concepts of sharing and receiving occur within the one realm of H_2O. One reality, but two intelligences. On this molecular level, they are indistinguishable.

The Endless World operates in similar fashion. It is total perfection—the Light sharing completely with the Vessel. The ultimate manifestation of sharing and receiving. Unity. Harmony. Infinite giving and receiving of fulfillment.

The Million-Dollar Question

What happened? Where is this Endless World?

How did we end up here, in this very problematic existence?

Why are we trapped on this side of the curtain where all is dark and dangerous?

If everything was unified and perfect in the Endless World, why are we reading this book in a world that is embroiled and flawed?

If we are part of the Vessel, why do we experience so much pain?

Where is the Light, the endless joy, the permanent happiness?

The DNA of God

Consider an empty glass. What happens when you fill it with hot water? The glass itself heats up. This is analogous to what took place in the Endless World. As the Light continued to fill the Vessel, attributes of the Light were passed on. We might even say that the Vessel inherited the nature of its Creator. This inherited nature is the power to create fulfillment, share fulfillment, and play an active and causal role in the ongoing process of Creation.

The God Gene:
Birth of a New Desire

Because the Vessel inherited the nature of the Light, a new desire arose within the Vessel. This new desire was a longing to express what might be called the DNA of God. Specifically, the Vessel wanted:

- To be the *cause* of its own happiness

- To be the *creator* of its own fulfillment

- To *share* fulfillment

- To *control* its own affairs

But because the Vessel could not express its "Creator genes," the Vessel no longer experienced infinite fulfillment. A lone desire remained unsatisfied. And that was a problem. Big time! Because infinite fulfillment was the reason the Vessel was created in the first place.

To find out what happens in this next phase of Creation, let's close the curtain on the 99 percent realm and turn our attention to a Little League baseball game taking place on a sun-soaked field during a warm spring day.

Field of Dreams

Bobby is nine years old. He's the pitcher on his Little League baseball team. If Bobby could have just one wish in the whole world today, it would be to pitch a ballgame that would fill his parents with pride and joy. Bobby is getting his chance today because his coach has selected him as the starting pitcher. And the little boy doesn't disappoint. He throws a no-hitter and sets a record for most strikeouts in a game.

After the final out, Bobby's teammates storm the mound, hoist him up on their shoulders, and parade him around the field in wild celebration. Bobby locks eyes with his parents, who are now beaming with delight in the stands. The emotions felt by this nine-year-old boy are indescribable.

After the game, Bobby discovers something rather shocking. It seems that his dad had made a prior arrangement with both coaches and both teams to throw the game for his son. It was Bobby's birthday, and his dad wanted his son to feel great on this special day. The entire game was fixed. From the first pitch to the last out. The hugs and cheers from his teammates were all staged. All because Dad wanted his son to experience those joyous feelings of victory and accomplishment.

How does Bobby feel now?

Think about it for a moment.

Bread of Shame

Bread of Shame is Kabbalah's term for all those dreadful feelings that little Bobby is experiencing. It's an ancient Kabbalistic phrase expressing all the negative emotions that accompany unearned good fortune. A down-on-his-luck man who is forced to accept charity from others is said to eat Bread of Shame. He has a deep-seated desire to earn the money needed to buy his own bread. He desperately longs to be in a situation where he can feed and support himself, not depend on the generosity of others.

One Lack

The Vessel had it all in the Endless World except for one thing: the ability to earn and be the cause of its own fulfillment.

Bread of Shame thus prevented the Vessel from experiencing absolute happiness.

This situation was certainly not the intent or thought behind Creation.

There was only one option: Remove Bread of Shame.

But how?

The Dilemma

As long as the Vessel did no more than receive, it remained unhappy. So, what could the Vessel do to remove those awful feelings known as Bread of Shame? Sharing was not an option, because there was nothing with which to share. There was only Light and Vessel unified in the Endless World. Perhaps the Vessel could share with the Light? A commendable idea, but the Light had no Desire to Receive. The Light is itself an infinite sharing force of Energy.

The solution:

The Vessel

STOPPED

receiving the Light!

Resistance

The ancient Kabbalists called the Vessel's act of pushing back the Light *Resistance*. This critically important word will come up again, so please remember it. The moment the Vessel resisted the Light from filling it, the Light constricted itself, creating a vacuum, a single point of darkness within the Endless World. The infinite had given birth to the finite.

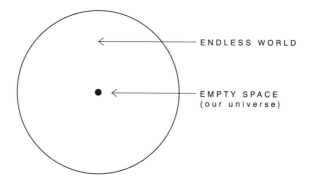

According to Kabbalah, it was a cataclysmic event that gave birth to the concepts of time and space as we understand them—an event that still reverberates to this day.

People of science have detected the cosmic echo of this explosion, and have dubbed it . . . *the Big Bang!*

The Big Bang

The idea that the ancient Kabbalists understood that a Big Bang explosion began our universe is intriguing, to say the least.

That Bang was actually confirmed by the NASA satellite COBE just a few years back. Newspapers and television newscasts around the world announced the discovery with great excitement. World-renowned physicist Stephen Hawking said it was the discovery of the century. Astrophysicist George Smoot said it was "like looking at God." Actually, it was more like looking at the Vessel's first effort to remove Bread of Shame.

Science, focused on the *hows* of physical reality, lacks the means to understand the spiritual significance of *why* the Big Bang occurred. Still, it's interesting to compare how ancient Kabbalah and 20th-century physics describe the beginnings of our universe. The similarities are remarkable.

Modern Science

Approximately 15 billion years ago, before the universe came into existence, there was nothing. No time. No space. The universe began in a single point. This point was surrounded by nothingness. It had no width. No depth. No length. This speck contained the whole of space, time, and matter. The point erupted in an explosion of unimaginable force, expanding at the speed of light like a bubble. This energy eventually cooled and coalesced into matter—stars, galaxies, and planets.

Kabbalah

The universe was created out of nothingness from a single point of light. This nothingness is called the Endless World. The Endless World was filled with infinite Light. The Light was then contracted to a single point, creating primordial space. Beyond this point nothing is known. Therefore, the point is called the beginning. After the contraction, the Endless World issued forth a ray of Light. This ray of Light then expanded rapidly. All matter emanated from that point.
— Kabbalist Isaac Luria, 16th century

Oh, and by the way, according to the calculations of the Zohar, the above Creation event *also* took place some 15 billion years ago.

Birth of a Universe

Like a loving parent who stands back to allow a child to fall so the child will eventually learn to walk, the Light withdrew the moment the Vessel said, "Thanks, but no thanks. I'd like to learn to create and share some Light on my own."

By withdrawing its radiance to create a point of emptiness, the Light gave the Vessel time and space in which to evolve its own divine nature through the act of finding the Light.

This microscopic point of emptiness, this newly-formed speck of space and time given to the Vessel is our vast, star-studded, physical universe.

The Surprise of Scientists and Scholars

The thought of science confirming what the Kabbalists already knew so long ago concerning Creation is surprising. But then again, it shouldn't be. After all, the Kabbalists also got their medical-science theories down right. For instance, the Zohar discussed the dangers of clogged arteries, plaque, and cholesterol in connection to the origin of heart disease some 20 centuries ago. But only in the last 60 years did medical science discover the same thing.

The Zohar also spoke about black holes in the cosmos and parallel universes. It described the earth as a circular sphere with different time zones some 1,600 years before science also concluded that our planet was not as flat as an ironing board.

Contemporary scholars and scientists are quite fascinated when they come across such speculations in the Kabbalistic writings of the Zohar. Internationally known mathematician, physicist, and best-selling author Dr. Amir Aczel was intrigued by Kabbalah's perspective on the origins of the universe. Aczel states:

As a scientist, I was extremely excited to discover through my research that there is a stunning similarity between physics and Kabbalah in regards to their descriptions of the universe and its creation!

Astrophysicist Bernard Haisch is the director of the California Institute for Physics and Astrophysics. Dr. Haisch's scientific research led to him to conclude that our entire physical world appears to be sustained at every instant by an underlying sea of quantum light. According to this astrophysicist, "Let there be light" is a very profound statement: Says Haisch:

The thing that strikes me most about the origin of the universe in Kabbalah is its emphasis on light. This reminds me of an underlying universal sea of quantum light called the electromagnetic zero-point field. Recent studies have uncovered the possibility of connections between this field and some of the fundamental properties of matter necessary for a physical universe to exist such as inertia, gravitation, and the stability of atoms.

Dr. Bruce Chilton is Bell Professor of Religion at Bard College. He is a biblical scholar, an Episcopal priest, and a best-selling author. Dr. Chilton has written extensively on the historical Jesus and his connection to the teachings of Kabbalah. In response to the Kabbalistic and scientific description of Creation, Professor Chilton states:

To recognize light as the initial act of creation is an insight as ancient as the book of Genesis, and physicists such as Stephen Hawking remind us that what is ancient is also current. But the breakthrough between science and Kabbalah, although significant, is only complete when you can see that the Light that is our origin is also the source of our breath and the ultimate goal of our striving

part three
the puzzle of creation, and the theory of reactivity

The Puzzlemaker

There once was a kind, old puzzlemaker who possessed magical powers. The puzzlemaker's greatest pleasure came from creating enchanting picture puzzles for the children who lived in his neighborhood. These puzzles were no ordinary puzzles. They had magical properties—when the final piece was snapped into place, beams of light would radiate from the images, filling the children with joy. All they had to do was gaze at the picture. Nothing more. For the kids, it was better than eating 10,000 chocolate chip cookies and drinking 10,000 glasses of milk.

One fine day, the puzzlemaker truly outdid himself. He painted his most spellbinding picture ever, using magical paints flecked with stardust and special brushes whose handles were encased in gold. The puzzlemaker was so excited by his creation that he decided not to carve the picture into individual puzzle pieces. Instead, he wanted the children to experience all the magic immediately.

As he finished packaging the picture, a little boy walked into the shop hoping to find the puzzlemaker's latest creation. The puzzlemaker excitedly handed over the package. The boy's bright-eyed smile quickly disappeared. His face turned a little sad. Clearly, he was disappointed at something. "What's wrong?" the puzzlemaker asked. The little boy explained that building and creating the puzzle was the actual fun part! The puzzlemaker understood immediately. And with as much love and care as he had put into creating the original image, the puzzlemaker cut and disassembled the picture. He lovingly scattered the

*individual pieces into the box. He then gave the children
what they really wanted more than anything else—the joy
and accomplishment of building the magical puzzle themselves.*

To provide the Vessel with the opportunity to create its own fulfillment, the Endless World was disassembled and transformed into
a picture puzzle. By allowing the Vessel to reassemble the puzzle
of Creation, we, the Vessel, become creators of our fulfillment and
the cause of our joy, thus fulfilling our deepest desire and most
profound need.

In addition to producing all these puzzle pieces, one more vital
element was required for the Vessel to truly become a creator of
Light . . .

The Power of Darkness

A burning candle emits no light against the backdrop of a brilliant sunlit day. The candle is worthless in this illuminated setting. But in a darkened football stadium, even a single candle is clearly visible and valuable. Similarly, the Vessel was incapable of creating and sharing in a realm already radiating Light. It was essential that an area of darkness come into being so that the Vessel could transform from a passive receiver into a being who genuinely earned and created Light and fulfillment.

Next question: So, how did the Light manage to hide its radiance?

A Ten-Dimensional Curtain

To conceal the blazing Light of the Endless World, a series of ten curtains were erected. Each successive curtain further reduced the emanation of Light, gradually transforming its brilliance almost to darkness.

These ten curtains created ten distinct dimensions. In the language of Aramaic, they are called the *Ten Sfirot.*

The Ten Sfirot

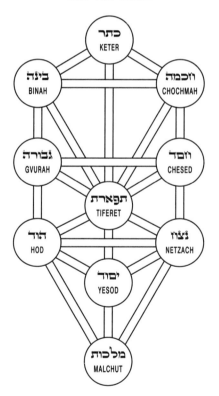

Keter, the top dimension, represents the brightest realm of Light, closest to the Endless World. *Malchut*, located at the bottom, denotes the darkest dimension, our physical universe.

The only remnant of Light in our darkened universe is a "pilot light" that sustains our existence. This pilot light is the life force of humanity. This pilot light is the force that gives birth to stars, sustains suns, and sets everything in motion—from beating hearts to swirling galaxies to industrious anthills.

Disassembling the Puzzle

A puzzle can only be a puzzle if there is *space* separating the individual pieces and *time* given to reassemble it.

The Endless World is a realm without time and space; therefore, the Light had to create them. This occurred *automatically* when the Light was hidden by the ten curtains.

Dimming the Light meant obscuring its true attributes:

- If Light exists on one side of a curtain, darkness must materialize on the other side when a curtain blocks out the Light.

- Likewise, if timelessness is the reality on one side of a curtain, the illusion of time is created on the other side.

- If there is perfect order on one side of the curtain, chaos exists in the other dimension.

- If there is wholeness and exquisite unity on one side of the curtain, then there is space, fragmentation, and the laws of physics on the other side.

- If God is a blatant reality and truth on one side of the curtain, then godlessness and atheism are the reality on the other side. (Thus, atheists would be correct in their viewpoint that there is no such thing as God. However, our uniquely human purpose in this world is to transcend our 1 percent realm and discover a higher truth, which is the subject of this book.)

Are you starting to get the picture? Welcome to our world of darkness and disorder!

The Deception of Darkness

Although we stumble around in the darkness and turmoil of this physical world, we can take heart, for in reality, the Light is still here! Cover a lamp with many layers of cloth and eventually a room becomes dark. Yet the lamp shines as brightly as ever. The intensity of the light never changed. What changed was the cloth covering the light. The Light of the Endless World works the same way. Kabbalah teaches us how to remove the layers of cloth one strip at a time to reassemble the puzzle of Creation and bring ever more Light into our lives.

Adam and Atom:
Partners in Creation

In a process whose description lies beyond the scope of this book, the one infinite Vessel broke into two distinct forces of spiritual energy: The male principle, called Adam, separated from the female principle, called Eve.

These two segments then shattered into countless pieces, creating male and female souls. The lesser sparks created the animal kingdom. All those sparks smaller than the animal kingdom formed the vegetable kingdom, all the way down to the fragments of matter and energy that make up the cosmos. So, everything from atoms to zebras, from microbes to musicians, is the result of this cosmic shattering. Everything is a portion of the original Vessel.

Adam had become atom. Or more precisely, Adam became the proton in an atom while Eve embodied the electron. These are the male and female energy principles that animate our universe.

Everyone's souls were part of the first, infinite, primordial Soul that split and shattered.

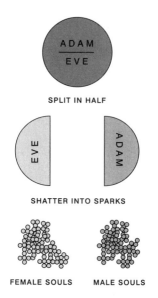

SPLIT IN HALF

SHATTER INTO SPARKS

FEMALE SOULS   **MALE SOULS**

Therefore, according to Kabbalah, everything in the universe is imbued with its own spark of Light, its own life force. Does this mean that even inanimate objects have souls? Does a rock have a soul? The answer is yes! The only difference between the soul of a rock and the soul of a rock star is the degree and intensity of their desire to receive Light.

The more Light an entity desires and receives, the greater its intelligence and self-awareness. A human being is more intelligent and self-aware than an ant, and an ant is more intelligent and self-aware than a rock.

Interacting Souls

Because the Vessel shattered into pieces, each individual spark of soul now has someone to share and interact with in order to accomplish the process of creating Light and reconnecting all the puzzle pieces.

So, now you know who you really are: You are a spark of the original shattered Vessel. So is your best friend and your worst enemy. Even the plants in your garden!

You also now know that your very essence, the actual stuff that you are made of, is *desire*. You desire Light. This means you desire happiness, wisdom, fun, fulfillment, peace of mind, well-being, and a whole lot of pleasure. All these elements of Light were hidden away so that you could become the *cause* of its illumination.

Before we reveal how we become the actual cause of our own Light, there is one more important phase of Creation that needs to be mentioned because it tells us precisely where this Light is, and how to access it at will.

Labor Contractions

At the precise moment of the Vessel's shattering, the ten dimensions underwent a sudden contraction in preparation for the birth of our universe.

Six of the ten dimensions enfolded into one and are known collectively as the Upper World.

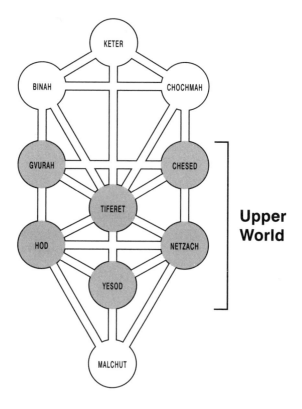

This contraction, according to Kabbalah, is the secret behind the phrase, *Six days of Creation*. Why, after all, would an all-powerful Creator require any amount of time to create a universe? God should be able to whip up a universe in less than a nanosecond!

Kabbalah agrees. The six days of Creation have nothing at all to do with the concept of time as we know it. It is a code for the uniting of the six dimensions into one.

Science Catches Up with Kabbalah

Two thousand years after the ancient Kabbalists revealed that reality exists in ten dimensions—and that six of those dimensions are compacted into one—physicists arrived at the same conclusions. This has come to be called Superstring Theory.

According to this theory, our universe is built of tiny, vibrating, string-like loops. Different vibrations of the string create different particles of matter.

Brian Greene, one of the leading string theorists, describes the theory in his book, *The Elegant Universe: Superstrings, Hidden Dimensions, and the Quest for the Ultimate Theory:*

> Just as the vibrational patterns of a violin string give rise to different musical notes, the different vibrational patterns of a fundamental string give rise to different masses and force charges. String theory also requires extra space dimensions that must be curled up to a very small size to be consistent with our never having seen them.

As it turns out, the number of dimensions required to make this theory work is ten. And, according to scientists, the number of dimensions that are curled up and compactified into one is six. These are identical to the numbers given by the ancient Kabbalists!

Dr. Michio Kaku is an internationally recognized authority in theoretical physics and a leading proponent of Superstring Theory. In his book *Hyperspace,* Dr. Kaku writes:

The Universe is a symphony of vibrating strings. And when strings move in ten-dimensional space-time, they warp the space-time surrounding them in precisely the way predicted by general relativity....During the Big Bang, six of the ten dimensions curled up (or "compactified") into a tiny ball, while the remaining four expanded explosively, giving us the Universe we see.

Dr. Kaku discussed the impact of this new (or old) idea on the scientific community. "To its supporters, this prediction that the Universe originally began in ten dimensions introduces a startling new realm of breathtaking mathematics into the world of physics," Dr. Kaku wrote. "To its critics, it borders on science fiction."

Dr. Kaku was surprised by the intriguing similarities between Kabbalah and the Superstring Theory. Says Kaku:

"It's eerie how the magic numbers of physics and the unified field theory are found in the Kabbalah!"

A Practical Science

What does all this intriguing scientific-Kabbalistic babble mean to us on a practical level? How do the events in our lives relate to an explosion that occurred some 15 billion years ago? Why should we care if the universe has 10 dimensions or 50 dimensions, for that matter? What does it have to do with the stresses in our own lives? Many rabbis, scholars, and scientists have acknowledged that there are profound similarities between Kabbalah, the Big Bang, and Superstring Theory. But so what? What's the relevance to our fears and phobias and desires for endless fulfillment? What's the connection to our unending urge for lasting happiness?

Therein lies the genius of Kabbalist Rav Ashlag: He synthesized these concepts and brought them down to the level where they could shed a profound light on their relevance to human happiness.

As stated earlier, the six dimensions that lie just beyond our perception are known collectively as the Upper World. The Upper World is the 99 percent realm that we spoke about in earlier chapters (see the illustration on page 86.)

- It is this 99 percent realm that we touch during those rare moments of clarity, rapture, mystical insight, expanded consciousness, a sixth sense, an epiphany, or tuning in to pick the winning numbers in the lottery!

- When Michael Jordan sank the winning shot to win the NCAA National Championship and launch his career, the joy he experienced emerged from this realm.

- When your heart beats like a drum and passion overtakes you when you first catch glimpse of your soul mate, you're touching the 99 percent.

- When you're lying on the beach with the sun splashing down on you and you haven't a care in the world, this almost supernatural serenity flows from worlds on high.

- Whenever you've felt pleasure, happiness, tranquility, inner peace, calmness, and the kind of confidence where you could conquer anything, you were touching one of the high levels in the Ten Sfirot.

As mentioned earlier, this is the realm Plato wrote about—the timeless world of Ideas or Forms that exists "beyond" the physical world of the five senses. Remarkably, Sir Isaac Newton, considered to be the greatest scientist ever, said that Plato borrowed these concepts from Kabbalah, using them to form his own views of reality. In one of his theological manuscripts, Newton wrote:

Plato, traveling to Egypt when the Jews were numerous in that country, learnt there his metaphysical opinions about the superior beings and formal causes of all things, which he calls Ideas and which the Kabbalists call Sfirot.

When we elevate ourselves and connect to this higher world, we bring lasting, positive change to our lives. Remember, move the arm that creates the shadow on the wall, and the shadow on the wall responds automatically. When we "move" the 99 percent, our 1 percent world follows suit.

How many times have we wondered, "Where's God when we need Him most?"

How many times have we asked ourselves why it's so difficult to connect with the Creator? The key to connecting to the Creator and having our prayers answered is knowing *how* to connect ourselves to the Upper World known as the 99 percent realm.

You will learn how to do that in the pages that follow.

The Theory of Reactivity

Everyone thinks of changing the world,
but no one thinks of changing himself.
　　— Leo Tolstoy

When we look into the realm of the 99 percent, we discover four key attributes of the Light that we inherited and need to express in our world in order to remove Bread of Shame.

They are:

- Being the *Cause*

- Being a *Creator*

- Being in *Control*

- *Sharing*

In our physical world, these four qualities merge into a single trait. My father, Kabbalist Rav Berg, elegantly expresses it in one word, directly relating to human behavior: PROACTIVE!

Further, all the traits of the Vessel—that is, of humanity—can be expressed in the single word:

Reactive!

Reactive means:

- Being the *Effect*

- Being a *Created Entity*

- Being *Under the Control of Everything*

- *Receiving*

Further Defining Reactive Behavior

Reactive behavior is founded upon the human Desire to Receive. This is the original desire that was created in the Endless World. Reactive behavior includes greed, selfishness, self-indulgence, anger, envy, and the like.

Reactive behavior is any reaction we have to external situations. This behavior can include resentment, jealousy, pride, low self-esteem, vindictiveness, and good old-fashioned hatred.

Take a moment and reflect upon these reactions. Recall the times when these emotions were provoked within you. Think about the situations that caused these feelings to come about.

In truth, 99 percent of our behavior is reactive. But that is by design. Remember, our essence is the *desire to receive* fulfillment.

Our consciousness is built on reactive, impulsive, instinctive desires. Rising above this consciousness constitutes genuine spiritual transformation.

Let's now examine how all these Kabbalistic concepts play themselves out in our real world.

The Meaning of Life

In simplest terms, the mission of the Vessel is to transform itself from being a reactive force into a proactive force. So, that means . . .

This is the ultimate purpose of life;

The reason for our existence;

The meaning of our lives;

This is the way back home;

The path to endless fulfillment;

The secret to removing Bread of Shame and expressing our godly DNA;

And the true definition of the term *spiritual transformation*.

We have now unveiled the Fourth Principle of Kabbalah:

The Purpose of Life Is Spiritual Transformation from a Reactive Being to a Proactive Being.

Deconstructing the Theory of Reactivity

- When we **react** to any external situations and events in our lives, we are merely an effect and not a cause; we are reactive, not proactive.

- Should we live our lives without any personal growth or change of nature, we are not **creating** new spiritual levels of existence for ourselves.

- When we allow outside forces to influence our feelings, positive or negative, we have surrendered **control**.

- When we exhibit egocentric or self-centered behavior, we are not **sharing** but instead receiving gratification for the ego.

Reflect upon this well before proceeding to the next page!

A Spiritual Big Bang

Whenever we react in life, whether in anger or with pleasure, the energy we feel is a dangerous *direct* connection to the 99 percent. This is the Light the Vessel first received in the Endless World. This Light gives us a burst of energy. A rush of pleasure. A feeling of gratification. However, it was also this initial glow of Light that gave birth to Bread of Shame! *The Vessel rejected this Light because it was received in a reactive manner.*

Whenever we behave reactively, we are denying our inherited godly nature. Our soul then replays the original act of Resistance and stops the Light from flowing. A spiritual version of the Big Bang is reenacted. Metaphorically, another cloth is flung over the lamp. Life gets darker. And that's when the pleasure wears off. The thrill leaves us. The rush is gone. This is why we feel so down after we've reacted and exploded in anger toward our spouses. This is why we crash after experiencing a "high" from drugs. This is why our excitement eventually dissipates after buying a new car or new clothes. The gratification or pleasure we drew was not created through our own proactive efforts. Something external was responsible for our fulfillment.

In the same way, if someone pays us a compliment and it makes us feel better about ourselves, the *other person* is the cause and we are just the effect. Our happiness will be only temporary. Our soul is forced to *reprise* the act of Resistance and cut off the Light to prevent Bread of Shame. Darkness is the eventual result.

A Spiritual Alternative

There is another option available to us that prevents "spiritual Big Bangs" from taking place in our life. This is the proactive use of Resistance, and it means stopping all of our reactive impulses through our own free-willed choice.

Although this can be expressed in one short sentence, accomplishing it requires almost superhuman willpower and self-restraint. We'll find out why it's easier said than done shortly. But first, try the following exercise to deepen your understanding of Resistance and learn what transformation truly means.

The $100,000 Quiz

Scenario Number One: *A hundred thousand dollars in small-denomination bills lies on top of a desk in a business. A man walks in and sees the money. He makes sure no one is watching, then scoops up the cash and flees like a bandit.*

Scenario Number Two: *A man walks in and sees the money. He begins shaking, fearing the prospect of even touching the cash, let alone stealing it. He flees the building like a scared rabbit.*

Scenario Number Three: *A man walks in and sees the money. He checks to see that no one is looking. Then he scoops up the cash and begins to flee. But he stops. He agonizes for a moment and decides to return the money to the desk.*

Scenario Number Four: *A man walks in and sees the money. He takes it and places it inside a briefcase. He locks the briefcase and hands it over to the authorities for safekeeping. He leaves a note on the desk that informs whoever has misplaced a large sum of cash to contact him and he will direct that person to the authorities to retrieve the money.*

Which scenario reveals more spiritual Light in our world? Which person expresses the most spiritual Light in his own life? Based upon all that we have learned, let's briefly examine each scenario to discover the answer.

Scenario Number One: In this case the man is governed by his reactive, instinctive Desire to Receive, which tells him to take the money and run. Reactive behavior produces no Light.

Scenario Number Two: This man is merely reacting to his

instinctive desire to be frightened by even the thought of stealing the money. Reacting to his natural instinct produces no Light. The man enters the building and leaves it again with his nature unchanged.

Scenario Number Three: The man initially reacts to his desire to steal the cash, but then he stops his reaction. He shuts it down, proactively. Then, going against his initial instinct, he transforms his nature in this one instant and returns the money. His transformation from reactive to proactive reveals spiritual Light.

Scenario Number Four: Here, the man merely reacts to his instinctive desire to do the right thing. He was already in a proactive state of mind concerning stealing the money. No change of nature occurs. He remains the same person throughout the situation. Such behavior produces no additional Light in this person's life, according to Kabbalah. The honorable man in this scenario can still reveal Light, however. After returning the money, he must not react to his ego, which is telling him how kind and virtuous he is. He must *resist* his Desire to Receive—which, in this case, means his *desire to receive praise for his good deed*. He must realize that the great opportunity is not the physical act of returning the money; it is keeping his good deed secret and rejecting self-praise.

Always remember that our positive traits do not flip on the Light switch. The Light goes on only when we identify, uproot, and transform our reactive negative characteristics. It is the degree of change in our natures that determines the measure of our fulfillment.

The Long Supermarket Line of Life

The next time you find yourself stuck in a long line at an ATM machine, traffic jam, or supermarket checkout counter, resist your urge to react. Do not get frustrated. Do not become impatient. Do not get angry. The line is there to test you, and to give you an opportunity not to react. If you do react, the situation controls you. The situation becomes the cause and you the effect.

Always remember that the reason for not reacting to the long supermarket line, the crazy driver who cuts you off on the inter- state, or your brother-in-law who irritates you to no end has noth- ing to do with being polite. Nor has it to do with good morals, ethics, or any other altruistic principle. It has to do with you, as in, *What's in it for you?*

Never about Morals

Historically, morals and ethics have never led to peace and unity. Morality might be a noble concept, but it won't ever change the nature of the beast. Never has, never will. We are a species of receivers, as in, *What's in it for me?* And that's okay. That was the Creator's intent.

In order to be motivated to take action, people must *receive something* in return. The purpose of Resistance is getting you closer to the Light so you *can* receive. So, stop your reactive desire to constantly think about yourself—not because this is morally good, but because the transformation will serve your interests. It's a paradox: When you stop thinking of yourself and you stop your receiving, the Light then thinks about you and you can receiving everything, *with no fear of losing it later!*

Each of us has the power to bring fulfillment to our lives by transforming our natures. When enough of us reach that level, the world will be overwhelmed with an unimaginable infusion of Light.

The Moment of Transformation

We have two choices in life:

1. React to a situation, in which case our souls will eventually resist the Light, leaving us in the darkness of the 1 percent realm.

2. Proactively resist our desire to react, thereby connecting ourselves to the 99 percent reality.

Option number two removes Bread of Shame, thus clearing the way for the Light to fill our lives in a particular circumstance. Put another way, the instant we resist a reaction, we have transformed a particular aspect of our selves—which happens to be the purpose of our existence. We automatically link up with the 99 percent, and the appropriate measure of Light radiates forth.

Hence, our Fifth Spiritual Principle states:

**In the Moment of Our Transformation,
We Make Contact with the 99 Percent Realm!**

The Transformation Formula

Changing reaction to proaction works like this:

1. An obstacle occurs.

2. Realize that your reaction—not the obstacle—is the real enemy.

3. Shut down your reactive system to allow the Light in.

4. Express your proactive nature.

The moment of transformation takes place during steps three and four. That is when you enjoin your soul to the luminous dimension of Light—the 99 percent realm.

Applying the Transformation Formula

Consider this scenario from life and watch how the formula works:

1. AN OBSTACLE OCCURS
Your friend blows up at you.

2. YOUR EMOTIONAL REACTION
You are upset. Angry. Hurt.

3. YOUR BEHAVIORAL REACTION
You yell back at your friend and stop speaking for months.

Analyzing the Transformation Formula

1. AN OBSTACLE OCCURS
Your best friend blows up at you.

2. REALIZE YOUR REACTION IS THE REAL ENEMY.
Your feelings of being upset, angry, and hurt are your real enemy—not your friend.

3. SHUT DOWN YOUR REACTIVE SYSTEM TO ALLOW THE LIGHT IN.
Let go of all your emotional reactions. Instead of shouting back and ending the relationship, take it all in. Even if you're not to blame, just let your friend vent. What matters is not who is right or wrong. What matters is your decision not to react.

4. EXPRESS YOUR PROACTIVE NATURE.
You are now in contact with the 99 percent. The emotions you will now feel and your next set of actions will be rooted in the Light. Automatically, positive feelings and behavior will come forth. You will see a surprising positive change in the external situation that was confronting you. Your friend will respond in a way you never dreamed possible. Or an enlightening piece of information concerning your relationship will suddenly come forth.

All too often, our attention is focused on external circumstances. Someone we love hurts us. A business deal falls through. We disagree with someone else's opinion. Someone insults us. A colleague gets the promotion that we deserved. A friend stabs us in the back. External events trigger reactions within us all day long. Instead of *reacting*, apply the formula. You'll see real miracles happen.

The Oldest Game

Imagine 18 people gathered on a baseball diamond. All of them are endowed with tremendous athletic talent, on the level of Joe DiMaggio, Babe Ruth, Sandy Koufax, and Alex Rodriguez. They are given all the equipment necessary to stage a ballgame: bats, baseballs, mitts, and bases. We even throw in a wad of chewing gum.

But suppose they were missing one vital ingredient—the rules of the game. These 18 people have never heard of baseball and have absolutely no conception of what it is. What would happen if all these players were told to play the game called baseball, and they were not allowed to leave the field until they were as capable as World Series champs?

Imagine the chaos! Fighting. Arguing. Frustration. Quitting. Some players might make up their own rules. Although the players are endowed with the attributes of baseball stars, all they can produce is pandemonium.

According to Kabbalah, it doesn't matter how much talent we possess. Without the rules of the game, the result is chaos. Which brings us to a game a lot older than baseball, and a lot more mysterious. The rulebook for this most challenging game was recorded in an ancient Kabbalistic manuscript some 2,000 years ago. The book is called the Zohar, and it contains all the spiritual secrets governing the game of life.

According to the wisdom of the Zohar, each one of us is a potential Babe Ruth in the game of life. Each one of us is born into this world with enormous talent. But for most of us, this talent remains untapped—because we've been playing the game without really knowing how it's supposed to be played. The result? We fight, we argue, we experience frustration, and we make up new games and play by our own rules each and every day. To no avail.

Kabbalah most definitely gives us rules, but without imposing constraints on our daily experience of the world. Instead, it presents a set of universal spiritual laws that liberate and empower us in body and soul. These laws are the 13 Kabbalistic Principles that are being presented throughout this book.

The Blindfold

Before we can begin to understand Kabbalah's spiritual principles on a deeper level, however, we must first overcome an obstacle. Those talented people on the baseball diamond now have a rulebook, but suppose we blindfolded them before they took the field. Even though they know the rules, they can't see. So, we've still got chaos!

According to Kabbalah, each of us comes into this world wearing a blindfold. Before we can continue to learn the rules of the game of life and truly act on them, we must first remove the blindfold and find out something rather important: *Who is our opponent in the game of life?*

Counterintelligence

Why does human nature seem so oriented toward self-destructive behavior? Why do we engage in activities that we know are bad for us, even when we don't want to? Why do we forsake what's good for us in favor of what's harmful? Why is greed more tempting and fun than generosity? Why is it so easy for us to get addicted to all things harmful? Why are good habits so difficult to develop? It's easy to get hooked on a brand-new chocolate desert on the very first bite. Yet it's nearly impossible to become habituated to steamed zucchini even after years of forcing it down our throats.

Anger, fear, jealousy, laziness—all our negative and destructive behavioral traits—are like the force of gravity. No matter how hard we try to jump ten feet in the air, we can't. Negativity constantly pulls us down, no matter how committed we are to breaking free. It's built into our nature. Likewise, gravitation toward good habits and positive traits never seems to take place. Instead, when it comes to all things beneficial, we're governed by the force of repulsion. There is a counterintelligence within us constantly sabotaging our efforts to change things for the better.

part four
**the game,
our opponent, and
the art of
transformation**

The *Other* Voice

You know how it is: You tell yourself, with deep conviction, that a diet and healthy living starts tomorrow. But when you're confronted with tomorrow—along with a cheese pizza—a second voice comes out of nowhere and pipes in. This second voice convinces you to put off your lifestyle change until *tomorrow*. It's as though you're programmed to fail when it comes to improving the quality of your life.

But we came to this world to change our nature! That's the deal that was struck in the Endless World. We, the Vessel, would no longer receive true and lasting fulfillment unless we removed Bread of Shame, unless we first transformed our reactive nature to proactive. This task is extremely difficult. In fact, it's almost impossible. Why is human nature so balanced toward the negative?

Why is a reactive response totally effortless and a proactive act practically impossible?

The Opponent

Real change is so hard because, as in every game, we are faced by an opponent in the game of life, one who constantly attempts to influence and control our behavior and subvert our lives.

We've learned that, because it inherited the DNA of God, the Vessel wanted to earn the Light and be the cause of its own fulfillment. One way to gain an even deeper understanding of this concept is to consider *the object of a game.*

In any athletic contest, the goal is to win. It doesn't matter if you're talking about the Los Angeles Lakers, Chicago Cubs, Miami Dolphins, New York Rangers, or a team playing in the Menomonee Falls Little League. If you ask someone what they're trying to accomplish, they will tell you it's to win the game.

But is this really the goal?

Suppose a Kabbalist invoked a magic formula that allowed your team to win every single game. No matter what happened, you always won. Game after game. Season after season. The outcome was always predetermined, and there was always the same guaranteed victory.

What would that really be like? You'd quickly discover that the game had become extremely boring. The incentive would be lost.

So, can we really say that winning is the ultimate goal? What we really want from a game is risk, challenge—and even the possibility of losing. More than winning, it's the test of our ability that makes it all worthwhile.

The concept of losing against an opponent is what gives definition, existence, and meaning to the concept of winning.

What Was Missing

We "had it all" in the Endless World, *except for one thing:* the ability to earn, deserve, and be the cause of the fulfillment that the Light bestowed upon us. So, we rejected the Light in order to become like the Light—to become the creators of our own fulfillment.

We wanted the opportunity to play the game of Creation on our own, to risk losing season after season, lifetime after lifetime, for that one chance to win it all and bring home the trophy. Only then could we ever possibly know genuine feelings of accomplishment and happiness. Only then could we truly maximize our power to be proactive. Without testing us to the highest possible degree, the godlike proactive seed within us would never fully blossom.

Like spiritual Olympic athletes, we must train ourselves mentally and emotionally so that our divine nature can evolve and manifest. This training satisfies our need to earn and create the Light in our life, and eradicate Bread of Shame.

The Company

A man builds a business from scratch into a multimillion-dollar corporation. After running the firm for 25 years, he decides to resign from his position as chief executive officer. He will become the chairman of the board, a position that is more honorary than hands-on.

Seeing that his daughter is blessed with talents equal to his own, the man awards his daughter 50 percent ownership in the firm as well as the position of CEO. But the promotion causes a problem for the young woman. Her father's blood, sweat, and tears—not her own—built the company, and although the father gave her the company out of love, admiration, and respect, the young woman feels as if she has received a handout.

The daughter would obviously love the half-ownership and the CEO position, but it has to be under the right conditions. So, she devises a plan. The company employs many thousands of people, so no one really knows who she is. She decides to apply for a job in the warehouse. She works hard for many months. After a while, she earns a promotion. Later, she earns another. She continues to work extremely hard over the years, and through countless hours of effort, determination, and her inherited head for business, she learns all facets of the operation as she climbs the ladder of success. Eventually, she works her way up to the top of the firm and becomes the president and CEO.

What's the difference between having stepped into ownership of the business and having risen through the ranks? The difference is, in her own mind, the daughter never really earned the ownership until she worked her way up from the bottom.

The daughter knew that once she achieved leadership through her own actions, she could enjoy everything her father intended for her. Furthermore, only through this process could the father's goal also be fully realized.

It's important to understand that at no time during the daughter's climb up the corporate ladder could her father have interfered. If his daughter had experienced any pain or setback, or even if she had been fired, the father would have had to stand back and allow his daughter to work things out for herself, no matter how painful that might have been.

But the father had faith in his daughter. After all, he raised her, and he knew that she was blessed with the same traits he himself had. He knew that once his daughter made it to the top, on her own merit, she would truly come to know and savor that wonderful feeling of achievement and fulfillment that comes from being an owner of the company.

In this story, the daughter is a metaphor for us—the Vessel—and the father is a metaphor for the Light. The Vessel needs to express its inherited proactive nature to remove Bread of Shame. To be proactive, we must first be reactive. And to be reactive, we need challenge. To make that transformation from reactive to proactive meaningful, worthwhile, and complete, we need a powerful opponent to test us.

Who is our opponent?

Internal Battle

Two thousand years ago, the Zohar revealed the Opponent. The Zohar even identified the various techniques, weapons, and strategies he uses. He is the unseen cause of chaos in the physical world and in the human spirit. His is the voice that whispers, "Eat the cake now. Start the diet again on Monday." It is he who arouses feelings of despair, pessimism, fear, anxiety, doubt, and uncertainty. He also stimulates overconfidence, ruthlessness, greed, jealousy, envy, anger, and vindictiveness.

The Opponent is the voice that says, "Go and do it!" even though we know we shouldn't. The Opponent is the voice that says, "Don't bother with it!" even though we know we should. And worst of all, even when we want to apply Resistance in our life and stop reactive behavior, our Opponent shrewdly talks us out of it.

For instance:

- You make a vow to start eating healthy foods—but the moment you see some junk food, the opponent coaxes you into putting it off another day.

- You promise to spend more quality time with your family—but something compels you to put in a 60-hour work week.

- You're driving and a passerby needs some assistance. Your initial thought is to stop and help—then your Opponent convinces you that someone else will probably help. You rush off to your lunch engagement as the Opponent rationalizes your unkind behavior the rest of the way.

- You make a commitment to save a little bit of money each month and become more fiscally responsible—but each month the Opponent convinces you to frivolously spend it all, justifying each expenditure in your mind.

- You walk into a health food store and spend a ton of money on vitamins of every kind, genuinely committing yourself to a daily regimen of nutrients. Six months later, the bottles sit half full on your shelf. Next year the same thing happens when you find yourself back in the health food store. This time you promise yourself it will be different—but it isn't.

- A close friend confides in you, sharing a personal secret. You promise your friend (and yourself) not to divulge it to anyone. A few days later, the Opponent nudges the words right out of your mouth while you're gossiping with someone else. You actually watch yourself spill the beans, even though, as the words roll off your tongue, you know you shouldn't be doing it.

- A dear friend moves into a nicer house than yours, or wears a new outfit or drives a sexy new car. You tell yourself to be happy for your friend, but envy begins to raise its ugly head and you cannot control the jealousy stirring inside of you, even though you want to. Resentment and happiness for the other person battle for control over your emotions.

An Ancient Adversary

Throughout history, religions, philosophers, and poets have given names to the Opponent, including Lucifer, Beelzebub, Mr. Hyde, the Evil Inclination, the Dark Side, Darth Vader, the Dark Lord, the Beast, and the Wicked Witch of the West!

Whatever you choose to call it, the ancient Kabbalists said the Opponent was real. Very real. Although you cannot see this Opponent with your eyes, he is as real as the invisible atoms in the air and as ubiquitous and influential as the unseen force of gravity. His true name in Aramaic, as revealed by the ancient sages of Kabbalah, is שָׂטָן. In English, this translates to "the Satan"—with the accent on the second syllable (suh-táhn).

The Satan is not the red-clad, double-horned demon who wields a mean pitchfork. These superstitions have only served to further conceal his true purpose and identity. His name is a code word for our ego. And our ego—the true Opponent— includes every form of reactive behavior.

Kabbalah says our Opponent is the ultimate master magician. His deceptive talents are best summed up by a line from the clever film *The Usual Suspects*, written by Christopher McQuarrie:

> *"The greatest trick the devil ever pulled was convincing the world he didn't exist!"*

He's Real!

There you have it, plain and simple. The Opponent is real and he exists as the human ego. But the Opponent does such a good job of hiding himself that we have forgotten and lost touch with our true selves—our souls. Instead, we are governed and ruled by the whims of ego, and the whole time we never realize we are being beaten and played by the Opponent.

We work 24/7 to fulfill the ego's every desire, no matter how shallow or self-destructive those desires may be. These impulses stemming from the Opponent control us 99.999 percent of the time.

The Opponent has fooled us into believing that we are victims of outside forces and other people's actions. He has convinced us that our enemy is some other person instead of our own reactive nature. All the while, he hides in the shadows of our minds, lurking in the dark recesses of our beings so we never know he exists. He inflates our egos so we think we're brilliant and in control of our lives. All the doubts we have about his existence are his doing.

Most important, he blinds us to our own godly nature so that we don't even recognize our purpose in life. Think about it. How many people do we really know who look inward each day, trying to uproot their negative reactive traits? Yet that is the true purpose of our existence.

And if you're still having a difficult time believing all this to be true, chalk up another one for the Opponent.

Altering our DNA

Desire to Receive attracts and draws energy. Desire to Receive can draw material and spiritual possessions for ourselves or for the sake of sharing with others as well. When the Opponent came into being, his appearance added another element to our natural *Desire to Receive*. It was as if our spiritual DNA had been altered, by adding a few more letters to the human genome. Those additional genetic letters are:

f.o.r. t.h.e. s.e.l.f. a.l.o.n.e.

Humanity was now imbued with a *Desire to Receive for the Self Alone*. This additional "selfish gene" comes from the Opponent. This is the singular root and motivating force behind humanity's reactive nature and our individual, impetuous, rash behavior. This is what makes the transformation from intolerant to tolerant so difficult.

The Desire to Receive for the Self Alone leaves not a scrap or morsel for anyone else. Like a black hole in deep space, this desire consumes everything within its vicinity so that even spiritual Light itself cannot escape its power.

The Difference Between Desire to Receive and Desire to Receive for the Self Alone

Desire to Receive is when we see another person's spiritual or physical possession, and a desire for the same possession is awakened within us. We then go out and acquire it. Fine. No problem.

But Desire to Receive for the Self Alone is when we attain a material possession, such as a car or a new designer outfit, and still we resent and begrudge our neighbor for buying the same item, even though it in no way diminishes our own possession. In other words, no one else should have but ourselves.

Our Opponent manipulates and controls our Desire to Receive for the Self Alone in several ways, starting with the Fields of Battle.

Fields of Battle

We discover that the Universe shows evidence
of a designing or controlling Power that has something
in common with our own minds.
　— Sir James Jeans, physicist

The battle against our Opponent has been going on for a long time, yet it takes place on a very murky, ill-understood terrain. This is the landscape of the human mind. But before we can truly understand what this means for us, we must understand what the mind really is.

> *Suppose a primitive tribesman ventures out of the jungle with no knowledge of the modern world. He comes across a transistor radio playing music and looks at it in astonishment, believing that the box is the source of the music. He opens up the radio and accidentally pulls out the transistor. The music stops. This convinces him that the radio is the source. In fact, he thinks he has killed the poor little creature. Of course, we know that the source of the music is really some radio station broadcasting over the airwaves from many miles away.*

Kabbalah teaches that our thoughts do not originate from the physical matter of the brain, just as music does not originate in the physical object of a radio. Instead, the brain is like an antenna, a receiving station that picks up a signal and then rebroadcasts it into the conscious mind.

During the 1950s, the brilliant neurosurgeon Wilder Penfield began extensive research into the mind-brain phenomenon. His goal was to explain how consciousness emerged from the physical matter of the brain. After 40 years of exhaustive study, Penfield admitted that he had failed. In *Mystery of the Mind* (Princeton University Press, 1975), a remarkable book detailing his decades of research, Penfield wrote:

> *The mind seems to act independently of the brain in the same sense that a programmer acts independently of his computer, however much he may depend upon the action of that computer for certain purposes. But who—or what—is that programmer?*

Ratings War

According to Kabbalah, two cosmic broadcasting stations—the Light and the Opponent—send signals to our brains. It's a ratings battle for the audience of mind—a bigger and far more important ratings battle than the three major networks have ever seen!

If we could learn how to distinguish which thoughts come from the Light and which thoughts originate from the Opponent, we could reclaim control of our lives.

A good starting point is this:

> *Any thought that is loud and crystal clear and urges us to react to a situation is the Opponent.*

Any thought that tells us that we are the architects of our own success and that we know better than the next guy is the voice of the Opponent. (The notion that our thoughts are chemical reactions in the brain is also the creation of our devious Opponent.)

> *If a thought is barely audible, a faint voice emanating from the recesses of our minds, it is the song of the Light. Or if what you have is a sudden flash of intuition or an impromptu inspiration, the broadcast is originating from that 99 percent realm.*

These two frequencies on the airwaves of our minds express themselves in this way:

- **The Opponent's thoughts manifest as our rational, logical minds and egos.**

- **The Light's signal manifests as intuition, dreams, and a faint quiet voice in the back of our minds.**

Usually, we are out of touch with our intuition. As a result, the Opponent rules the airwaves of the mind and plays one particular hit song over and over again—the song called *Reaction!*

The secret to taking control of our lives is to cut off the Opponent's signal. When we stop our reactive impulses, we literally turn off his broadcast.

When we succeed at this, even for a moment, the Light's signal is free to fill that space. Our lives and our decisions are rooted in infinite wisdom. Automatically, we make the right choices. The right thoughts come to our minds. The perfect words are spoken. Proactive emotions appear. The best ideas come forth at once. We suddenly see the deep-seated wisdom in an opposing argument put forth by a colleague, friend, or spouse.

But to prevent this from happening, our Opponent has some cutting-edge strategies and some state-of-the-art weaponry at his disposal.

Tactics

The Opponent's sole objective is to arouse our Desire to Receive for the Self Alone so that we disconnect from the Light and the 99 percent. His major tactic is to simply push our reactive button all day long. When this button is pushed, we are consumed with negative thoughts, selfish impulses, and egocentric urges to fulfill our Desire to Receive for the Self Alone.

Thus, we lose touch with our essence, our soul. Another cloth is placed over the lamp. The curtain between the 1 percent and the 99 percent grows thicker. There is more darkness in our lives. From this darkness emerges chaos.

But when we proactively reenact the original Resistance—performed by the Vessel in the Endless World—by refusing to react, we are pulling an emergency lever that overrides the reactive button that the Opponent pushed. This lever activates a shutoff valve that immediately cuts off the reactive emotions flooding our bodies. We are no longer reactive. We are proactive. We have made contact with our souls and the 99 percent. And that is when the Light on the other side of the curtain shines into our lives.

But like any worthy adversary, the Opponent returns for round two.

What's Up Is Down, What's Down Is Up

Kabbalist Rabbi Yehuda Ashlag, the 20th-century mystic, said that people usually perceive events to be exactly the opposite of their true state of reality because of their limited view of reality. To illustrate the point, he offered this simple thought experiment:

> *Imagine a person who has lived in total isolation since birth. He's never observed a living creature, either human or animal, in his entire life. Placed before him are a newborn hippopotamus and a newborn human baby. He observes the two. The baby obviously cannot take care of herself. She cannot crawl, let alone walk, and must be carried from place to place. She cannot communicate her needs clearly, or even feed herself. The baby doesn't fully perceive her surroundings. If a fire erupted near her, for instance, she would not even sense the danger. Basically, the newborn is helpless. But the baby hippo immediately perceives his environment. He knows to run from fire. He can feed himself. Within five minutes of birth, the newborn hippo can walk and swim.*

What conclusion would our isolated observer draw? Probably he would believe that the hippo was a more advanced creature than the baby. By contrast, Rav Ashlag taught that the more advanced a creature is at the beginning of growth, the less developed it will be at the end. Conversely, the less advanced a creature is at the beginning of its development, the more advanced and evolved it will be by the end.

The same principle is at work in all areas of life. Opportunities that look promising at the outset turn out to be disasters, while seemingly hopeless situations unexpectedly prove to be blessings in disguise. We misjudge situations because we lack the ability to perceive both the short-term effects and the long-term outcome. We react to the moment.

Kabbalah teaches that, more often than not, the final outcome of any life process will be the exact opposite of the first impression. Our Opponent tries to reverse this spiritual truth by inciting reactions to the present moment. He limits our ability to calculate and consider long-term consequences by igniting immediate responses to everything our eyes see and our ears hear.

And while we are in the throes of a reaction, the Opponent goes into his arsenal and pulls out *yet another weapon*.

The Weapon of Time

Time is an illusion. It's a phantasm created, in part, by the five senses. "Yesterday," "today," and "tomorrow" are actually enfolded into one unified whole. This is an engaging intellectual concept. But for some unknown reason, we cannot revisit the memorable moments of yesterday, we still fail to foresee the events of tomorrow, and a lot of us can barely cope with the present. That makes for one impressive illusion.

The fact of the matter is, physicists have absolutely no idea what time really is or why it bothers to exist. Go ahead and ask them. The greatest minds of science will admit that they haven't yet figured out time. What they do know is that time is like an elastic band that can be stretched or contracted. But why time is part of our reality—for that they have no clear-cut answer.

Well, you're now going to discover what the greatest minds of science could not: the true definition and purpose of time according to the Zohar.

First, what is time:

- Time is the distance between cause and effect.

- Time is the separation between action and reaction.

- Time is the space between activity and repercussion, and the divide between crime and consequence.

Why Time Exists

Without time, we would be instantly penalized the moment we reacted. Likewise, an immediate reward would appear with each positive deed and transformation of character.

Here's the problem with that kind of "timeless" instant feedback: Animals can be taught to behave in a certain manner through *immediate response training*. A dolphin will perform a spectacular double flip for a handful of tasty, tiny fish. A poodle will stop leaving puddles on the carpet if reprimanded each time there's an "accident." But that is reactive behavior—reacting to immediate external stimuli. Worse, it's blind, robotic behavior, the exact opposite of a free-thinking soul cut from the same cloth as the Divine.

Within this gap between cause and effect, we hope to become enlightened to the senselessness of our negative reactive ways and to recognize the rewards associated with spiritual growth and positive, unselfish, proactive behavior.

But it's up to each individual to gradually learn such lessons on our own, for time bestows upon us the greatest gift ever given:

Free Will

Our unique mission in the world is to elevate to a higher spiritual level. Thus, we are imbued with the divine-like feature of "free will" when it comes to changing our ways and ascending the spiritual ladder. Free will *only* occurs if the concept of time is injected into our existence.

There's a downside to all this: Because of time's existence, we mistakenly believe that goodness goes unrewarded while wickedness goes unpunished. But it's merely a delay tactic.

Delayed responses permit freedom of choice between good and evil behavior. Keep in mind, evil behavior encompasses much more than just murder. A few unkind words to your neighbor, spouse, or friend sets the cause-and-effect principle into motion, as well. In fact, assassinating a person's character is often as destructive as committing a physical homicide, according to Kabbalah. One destroys the body, but the other damages the soul. We can kill someone physically, or we may also kill someone emotionally and spiritually. We can destroy someone's relationship, or we may also ruin their livelihood.

The sin of "spilling blood" is not limited to physical violence. *Spilled blood* also refers to the shame or embarrassment we cause people by forcing blood to rush to their faces out of humiliation when we demean them in front of others. All of these unkind actions launch a cause-and-effect chain reaction.

Here's how it all works:

A person reacts and commits a misdeed. According to the law of cause and effect, there should be an immediate negative payback. However, a chunk of time is now tossed into the cause-and-effect process by our Opponent so that the negative payback is *delayed*. The person now believes he or she got away with the hurtful action.

This distance between cause and effect prevents us from perceiving the connections between the events of our lives. We might have planted a negative seed 30 years ago, but by the time it sprouts, we have forgotten about the seed. Eventually, a tree (chaos) "suddenly" appeared out of nowhere. Yet nothing happens by chance. Everything can be traced to some seed planted in our past. Time just makes us forget the original causative action. Chaos appears sudden because time has separated cause from effect.

Time creates the illusion of chaos when, in fact, there is a concealed order.

Time Reactive

Our five senses prevent us from seeing through the illusion of time and so we react to time's influences in other ways. Consider time-related concepts such as past, present, and future

> **Yesterday:** All too often we find ourselves clinging to yes-terday. We are prisoners to feelings of regret, vengeance, resentment, and other destructive emotions rooted in our past. We harbor these feelings and let them damage our lives in the present.

> **Today:** Many of us find it tempting to run from the challenges and pressures of the present moment. So, we procrastinate and put things off. We create false hopes about the future and live in denial about our current situation.

> **Tomorrow:** We are filled with anxiety about what will be. We are frightened by the unknown future, terrified by tomorrow. We are not sure which decisions to make or what the outcomes of our choices will be. Fear and trepidation consume us.

All these feelings are reactions—because we have allowed time to control our lives.

When, however, we *resist* our reactions to time, we suddenly become master over it. And that's when we gain the ability to bend time and manipulate it. We can slow it down or speed it up, defying all logic and our rational senses. Kabbalists throughout history were renowned for controlling time in ways that Einstein could only imagine. In fact, if not for Einstein, the notion of time being an illusion would be flatly rejected. Such a claim would be considered mysticism and science fiction. Albert showed otherwise.

Time Is One

It seems to us that the past is gone and the future is not yet here. Yet past and present are always with us. Two thousand years after the ancient Kabbalists revealed this concept, Einstein made similar assertions. It's only the limits of our consciousness that prevent us from perceiving yesterday—and tomorrow—right now!

But how can past, present, and future all exist at once?

Here is another thought experiment:

> *Imagine a 30-story building. We are now standing on the 15th floor, which represents the present moment. Floors 1 through 14 represent the increments of time that brought us to this moment. Floors 16 through 30 represent the future of our lives.*
>
> *What do we currently perceive with our five senses?*
>
> *Only the 15th floor.*
>
> *We cannot see the floors below, and we cannot see the floors above.*
>
> *Yet all the floors—that is, past, present, and future—exist as one unified whole: the entire 30-story building. And if we could float outside the building's 15th floor and look at it from a distance, we could see all 30 stories at once!*

That's a nice abstract concept to engage the mind, but what's the lesson for our lives? Who cares if time is really one? Who cares if tomorrow is here right now? We can't see tomorrow and we can't perceive yesterday, so what good does that information do us?

Good questions, and the answers teach us an important lesson.

The Test of Time

When we behave proactively, the Opponent uses time against us to sabotage our accomplishments. Just as the chaos may be delayed, the Light due us may also be delayed. If we think we've been proactive, but find ourselves wondering when we'll get the Light, our adversary has won another round. It was just a devious delay tactic to incite us into reacting with doubt and disbelief.

If we apply Resistance in a situation and our Opponent throws a bit of time into the process, the spiritual Light owing might not shine immediately. Consider the delay an additional test to make sure our proactive response was genuine and deep. If we react to the delay, we lose.

Thus, time is further defined as the distance between good deeds and their dividends. Just as time is the distance between crime and punishment, it is also the space between Resistance and reward.

Tricks with Time

It can get even trickier: Suppose there is a wonderful reward in store for someone, because of a positive proactive deed he or she committed some ten years prior. Follow this carefully: Now, at the precise moment of a new negative misdeed, the Opponent takes *time* out of the cause-and-effect process relating to the prior positive action. What happens? All of a sudden, a reward falls into the person's lap right after committing the negative act. It appears as though this person received Light for the wrongful behavior. It looks as if this person got away with the crime and actually benefited in other areas of his or her life.

Or consider this scenario: A person decides to *resist* a negative reactive urge. Instead, this individual chooses to be proactive and perform a positive deed. But then, the negative payback that is due from a prior reactive action suddenly stares him or her in the face. Why? How? Simply because the chunk of time that was delaying the prior judgment is immediately removed from the process by the crafty Opponent. So, after having performed a wonderful act of kindness, life suddenly gongs this person on the head.

This creates the fantastic illusion that life lacks true justice and that goodness doesn't pay. This whole chaotic view of reality occurs because we are shortsighted people who allow time to rule and dictate our lives. We live and die by the moment and the urge to immediately and constantly gratify our reactive impulses born of ego.

Time to Pay the Piper

Guess what? Every one of us faces the consequences of our negative actions, large and small, at some point in the future. You can bet on it. It could take months. Years. Decades. Even a few lifetimes, according to the ancient Kabbalists.

And this is one reason why life all too often appears maddening, chaotic, random, and totally out of control.

By the way, free will is so precious a gift, you even have the free will to doubt all these Kabbalistic truths concerning time, justice, payback, and cause and effect. And the Opponent will be there every step of the way telling you that these are nice intellectual concepts to read about in a book, but hardly believable or practical out in the real world. *(He's good, isn't he!)*

The Weapon of Complacency

Spirituality, according to Kabbalah, is *not* about trekking up a mountain to commune with God and nature while meditating alongside a clear stream as the birds sing the beauty of the world. That makes for a poetic scene, but it is not the purpose of our lives. Nor is divorcing ourselves from the physical world, secluding ourselves up on a mountaintop contemplating the majesty of nature. According to Kabbalah, these are *not* effective ways to achieve spiritual growth.

We came down from the mountain, so to speak, to enter the world of chaos, hardship, turmoil, and burden so we could confront the triggers that ignite reactions. Each trigger gives us the opportunity to transform our reactive behavior and become the cause of our fulfillment. Transformation. That's how we rebuild the puzzle of Creation. Like an old proverb says,

Smooth seas do not make skillful sailors.

In truth, our positive traits do not win us any points in life. Our wonderful characteristics and endearing qualities serve no practical purpose when it comes to arousing new levels of fulfillment and Light in our lives. Those traits are *already* in a proactive state. On the contrary, it is our negative characteristics and traits that give us the opportunity to effect a true transformation of character.

We came to this world to create positive change within ourselves and the world around us. Positive change will *always* encounter resistance, conflict, and obstacles. We must embrace these difficult situations. A man can live in a small town, in a modest house with a white picket fence and a wonderful garden that he tends all day long. It's a good life, a tranquil life. At age 95, he passes on peacefully in his sleep. On the surface, it appears to be an ideal existence. But was this really his purpose on this planet? Was there any internal change in this man's life? Is he a different, more evolved spiritual being at age 95 than he was at 35 or 65?

Some people live 70 years as if it were one day. Some people live one day as if it were 70 years. The white picket fence, early retirement, the simple lifestyle—all of this leads to complacency. These things can be weapons of our Opponent, who will instill complacency within us to prevent us from making inner changes. Then, when it's too late, we realize that life was empty, without meaning, and we made no impact upon this world.

Even worse, some people go to their graves without realizing that their existence was empty.

The Weapon of Space

What about all those people who actually seem to succeed with reactive, selfish behavior? Well, *seem* is the key word. Our actions in one area of life seem to have no relationship to consequences in other areas. This creates a marvelous illusion of space and separation, and the Opponent takes full advantage of it. If we're sharks in business, the Opponent has the power to *redirect* chaos toward our family life. If we are deceitful toward our spouse, the Opponent can have the payback directed toward our business.

Ninety-nine percent of the time, our wants and desires are implanted by the Opponent. Conversely, when the Light we generated by our proactive behavior in business materializes in our personal life, the Opponent will keep us preoccupied with business. When the Light does not materialize as increased profits, we assume that our proactive behavior is not working. We will *not* notice that our children are suddenly feeling a stronger spiritual bond with us. Or perhaps a serious undetected illness has *vanished* by our revelation of Light.

The Opponent limits our view and focuses our attention on situations that fuel our egos, so we fail to appreciate and receive the richness life offers us and the hidden blessings we receive daily.

The other way in which the Opponent uses space is through the concept of *place*. Space creates a place for the Opponent to live. Each time we react, we disconnect from the 99 percent. This disconnection creates a space, a void, and the Opponent uses that space as a place to stir up chaos. The bigger the space, the greater his presence and the larger the chaos. The bigger our reactions are, the greater space we create for our Opponent.

This is why a picture puzzle has order and meaning when it is fully assembled. There is no space between the puzzle pieces. Adding space between the individual parts creates disorder and chaos. The more space, the more chaos. A cancerous tumor becomes a problem because it expands and takes up more space. Chemotherapy shrinks the tumor and thereby shrinks the space.

There is only ONE way to genuinely remove space: *remove* the separation between us and the 99 percent.

How?

We achieve that by *connecting* to the 99 percent. And we accomplish that by *disconnecting* from reactive behavior!

Nanotechnologists Confirm the Kabbalists

Scientists on the cutting edge of nanotechnology are reaching the same conclusions about space as did the ancient Kabbalists. Briefly explained, nanotechnology refers to the science of manipulating atoms and molecules—something that was once considered unthinkable. The term *nano* refers to a nanometer (nm), which translates into one billionth of a meter or one millionth of a millimeter. To get some sense of this, three to five atoms fit within one nanometer. We are talking about the smallest possible space. Working at this level has the potential to yield benefits such as pollution-free manufacturing, invisible computers, super-strong materials, and microscopic machines that could roam through a person's body and repair a defective heart atom by atom.

We see the benefits of "less space" in other areas of technology as well. As space shrinks and physical matter is reduced, technology becomes more powerful. Consider the first transatlantic telephone cable. This bulky line carried approximately 32 phone calls. You might assume that to add more callers, one must simply enlarge the cable. That was the old way of thinking. Today, scientists recognize that less matter and less space, not more, equal more raw power. A micro-thin fiberoptic cable carries 320,000 phone calls on a simple thread of light. Dazzling.

Let's use an extremely simple analogy to further convey the problems of space. Consider the following array of letters:

HAPPINESS

This sequence spells out "happiness." But if we add a single space in the middle of the word, the entire meaning of the word becomes invalid. It no longer makes any sense. It becomes chaos.

HAPP INESS

So how do we remedy chaos? Simply remove the space, and chaos becomes happiness. The difference between a scientist and a Kabbalist is that a scientist still uses physical tools—albeit tiny ones—to manipulate an atom with nanotechnology. Anything physical still concerns space, and space always includes the Opponent. A Kabbalist manipulates atoms with consciousness and Light. And because there is no space in the Light, there is no Opponent to muck things up. When we shut down our reactions, all space vanishes as we achieve unity with the Light in that one moment. The Opponent is homeless. All the atoms around us follow the guidance of our soul, as opposed to the will of our Adversary. As we strengthen our consciousness with the Light and wisdom of Kabbalah, our ultimate destiny will be total control over space, time, and matter. Kabbalah is nanotechnology in its purest form. Without a doubt.

The Weapon of Disguise

One of the Opponent's most potent weapons is the ability to confuse us. We feel sad and disoriented, angry and envious, and we never know who our real opponent is.

In the course of all the mergers and acquisitions, all the takeovers, deal cutting, wealth building, promotions, job changes, spousal fights, divorces, lawsuits, bypass operations, backstabbing, gossiping, bad-mouthing, rationalizing, justifying, and blaming, we think the opponents are our neighbors, our enemies, and our friends whom we feel compelled to outdo with our cars, homes, clothes, and holidays. Or we think the opponent is our business competitor. Or the person at work who gets all the credit for the work we do. Or maybe the opponent is the whole rotten world, the whole corrupt system that has failed us and done us wrong. Maybe that's why our lives are so miserable.

But it isn't so. The Opponent is a master magician. A master of disguise. The Opponent projects himself onto other people so you recognize all of your faults in others and see the enemy as the other person. In reality, you're playing against the Opponent and *don't even know it.* You even doubt his existence *right now,* while reading a book on Kabbalah that plainly identifies him!

When someone wrongs you and you react, you lose. Even more remarkable, according to Kabbalah, *you deserved to be wronged by that person* because of a negative deed you committed previously in some area of your life. It is a critically important proactive behavior to remember this difficult truth the next time life gongs you over the head.

Hence, the Sixth Kabbalistic Principle states:

**Never—and That Means Never—Lay Blame
on Other People or External Events.**

Unmasking Our True Adversary

Here's a very powerful and practical technique to help you put this rule into action. Whenever someone does something really rotten to you, imagine that you can actually see the Opponent whispering in that person's ear, causing all their negative behavior, which by the way, is exactly what's happening! See the person in front of you as a helpless puppet under the complete influence of the Opponent. Recognize him as the culprit. Know that he is laughing at the two of you as he tries to fan the flames of hatred and conflict between you.

How do you feel now? This should help alleviate your reactive emotions toward this person, putting you in a better frame of mind for the real transformational work that begins when you look inward. Then you can see that *the Opponent was whispering in your ear, too.* All your negative feelings were being provoked by *his* suggestions. He was helping you project all your negative traits onto the other person the whole time. In fact, you were able to recognize and react to negative traits in others *only* because you have them yourself.

Resistance and Short Circuits

When Kabbalists speak of Light with a capital *L*, they are referring to the infinite Light of the Creator, the source of all our fulfillment. When Kabbalists speak of light with a lower case *l*, they are referring to sunlight or the light of a bulb. Both *light* and *Light* share similar characteristics concerning illumination.

Do you know how a light bulb works? Inside are three components:

    1. A positive pole (+)

    2. A negative pole (–)

    3. A filament separating the (+) from the (–)

Of the three components, the filament is the most important. It acts as a *resistor*, pushing back the current flowing from the positive and preventing it from connecting directly with the negative. This resistance, or pushing back of energy, is the reason the bulb generates illumination. When the filament breaks, the positive connects *directly* with the negative and the bulb short-circuits. It bursts, producing a momentary flash of light. But then there is darkness. In other words, without resistance, there is no lasting Light.

The Light Bulb Metaphor Applied to the Endless World

- The negative pole in a light bulb corresponds to the Vessel.

- The positive pole corresponds to the Light.

- The filament corresponds to the Vessel's act of Resistance, which caused the Big Bang.

At the moment the Vessel resisted and stopped receiving the Light in the Endless World, it changed from a reactive to a proactive state. From that act of *Resistance* were born the rules for revealing both *light* and *Light*.

The Light Bulb Metaphor Applied to Life

- The negative pole in a light bulb corresponds to our reactive desires.

- The positive pole corresponds to all the fulfillment and Light we seek from life.

- The filament corresponds to our free will to choose NOT to react, thus avoiding direct pleasure.

Just as the resistance of the filament keeps the light aglow in a bulb, resisting our reactive behavior keeps spiritual Light shining. When we fail to apply Resistance to our reactive impulses and we react, we create a short circuit. A direct connection occurs between our reactive desire (the negative pole) and the Light of pleasure (the positive pole). There is a momentary flash of self-indulgent delight followed by darkness, because the "bulb," the soul, has short-circuited and burned itself out.

A Universe of Resistance

The concept of revealing Light through Resistance is present in every area of our lives. When we listen to a violinist play an instrument, sound waves are created by the Resistance of the bow against the strings. We perceive the music when our eardrums *resist* the sound. That is the seemingly magical creative power of Resistance.

In a similar way, we've all seen those breathtaking images of the earth from space. Like a sparkling blue jewel, the earth radiates gloriously against the velvety blackness. Once again, the principle of Resistance is responsible. The earth's atmosphere *resists* the sun's light, creating illumination. But the void of space produces no Resistance whatsoever, and the result is darkness, although sunlight fills the vacuum.

Human beings possess free will to *resist* the pleasurable energy generated by reactive impulses. Free will can occur only if something terribly influential tries to persuade us not to resist—therein lies the purpose of the Opponent and the obstacles he throws our way.

The Seventh Principle of Kabbalah states:

Resisting Our Reactive Impulses Creates Lasting Light.

The Eighth Principle of Kabbalah states:

Reactive Behavior Creates Intense Sparks of Light,
But Eventually Leaves Darkness in Its Wake.

Suppressing vs. Resistance

There is a very fine line between suppressing our emotions and shutting down our reactive systems. Suppressing emotions creates long-term stress. Slowly, suppressed emotions gather force. Pressure builds, and eventually we blow!

Resistance, on the other hand, creates momentary struggle, but almost immediately there is calm and clarity. For example, if someone angers us and we truly apply the Kabbalistic concept of Resistance toward our usual rash response, there is no animosity. No vengeance in our hearts. We do not feel insulted or hurt. If we feel any of those things, if we get caught up in the drama of the moment, it means that we have failed to recognize the spiritual opportunity of the situation. That's our clue.

When we recognize that anger and other negative emotions are just tests sent to us by the Light so we can remove Bread of Shame, we will know with certainty that we applied Resistance. We will feel the resplendent presence of the Light that has emerged from our transformational action. We will *know*.

At first, the effort to resist will be a combination of suppression and authentic Resistance. That's okay. This effort will gradually remove layers of reactive emotions. Consistent efforts at Resistance will progressively cleanse reckless behavior, selfish desires, and negative thoughts from our nature. *Certainty* that we are drawing Light, and *awareness* of the process, are just as important as our attempts at Resistance.

Resisting our reactive emotions is refined and perfected as we continue to undertake it. We become more proficient as we experience this process and internalize these Kabbalistic principles.

Coping vs. Resistance

When we resist the urge to react and create a space for the Light to enter our beings, this spiritual energy has a transforming and purifying effect on our consciousness. For instance, merely *coping* with an anxiety attack will not remove deep-seated fear or prevent an attack from recurring.

Resistance, however, will accomplish this feat. When we apply Resistance with the conviction and intent to remove Bread of Shame, our actions now strike at the seed of the problem. Namely, knowing with deep trust that we are transforming from reactive to proactive will generate Light. This Light will illuminate the unseen root cause of our anxiety. Moreover, this Light will also cleanse and correct the cause and gradually eliminate panic from our life. In the dimension of the Light—in that other reality—negativity has no part. Through Resistance, we can enter that realm to uproot, cleanse, and eradicate anxiety from our being.

Ronnie (not his real name) studied Kabbalah for approximately six years. He shares his own experience with severe anxiety attacks and illuminates the difference between Resistance and coping:

> *Prior to Kabbalah, I couldn't drive far from my house without experiencing a terrifying panic attack. I would hyperventilate and was sure I was going to stop breathing. When I had to fly, I doped myself up on Dramamine and Ativan tranquilizers. If I had to drive far, I took half an Ativan. My life came to a standstill. Then I began behavior therapy treatment. It helped me to cope my way through the attacks. Eventually, I didn't have to take the pills, but I needed them in my back pocket to give me an escape and a sense of security. That, combined with relaxation*

techniques, helped me contend with my anxiety. But I was still compromising. I was surviving. I wasn't truly living.

Then I came across Kabbalah. Learning Kabbalah, practicing its various tools, including Resistance, helped me get to the root cause of my problem, which was spiritual, not physical. There was a period of cleansing, purifying, dealing with personal issues, going through a healing crisis, but then it was over. What totally amazed me, beyond words, was that it was as though the entire memory and experience of anxiety was erased from my consciousness. I remember the first time I sat on a plane—a five-hour flight from New York to Los Angeles—without any tranquilizers in my system or in my pockets. I totally let go. On the flight, there was no need for relaxation techniques. No fearful thoughts or anticipation. Nothing. There wasn't even the usual high you get when you overcome an attack. It was totally uneventful because I was now a normal (spiritual) human being who had completely erased the underlying cause of his anxiety attacks from his soul.

The Joy of Obstacles: An Alternative View of Life's Challenges

As we've learned, spiritual transformation does not mean seeking refuge from the problems of life by lighting incense and chanting away our cares. Rather, we must confront our chaos and our reactions to it.

To help us receive more spiritual Light into our lives, Kabbalah offers us the Ninth Principle, which states:

**Obstacles Are Our Opportunity
to Connect to the Light.**

The more barriers there are, the more chances we have to plug in to the Light. The more obstacles, the greater the number of triggers to ignite our reactions, so that we can *resist* and transform them. The more, the merrier! After all, *transforming* is the purpose of our lives (see Kabbalah's Fourth Principle), and *only* an obstacle can give us that opportunity!

When Bigger Is Better

The Resistance we apply in a situation also determines *how much* Light we receive. Imagine a tiny stone in space. It reflects and generates an amount of light relative to its size. Suppose we put a 50 x 50-foot sheet of mirror in space. More resistance and reflection occurs; therefore, more Light is revealed.

This simple principle is the key to determining how much spiritual Light we generate. The more Light we reflect, the more we receive. The more we *resist* our reactive behavior, the more happiness and pleasure radiate in our lives.

It works like this:

- The bigger the problem, the stronger our urge to react.

- The bigger our reaction, the more Resistance we have to apply to stop it.

- The more Resistance we apply, the more spiritual Light in our lives.

So remember the following Tenth Principle the next time a formidable challenge looms on the horizon:

**The Greater the Obstacle,
the Greater the Potential Light.**

The Path of Most Resistance

Most people tend to choose the path of least Resistance in life. They look for the easy, comfortable situations. But staying comfortable doesn't generate lasting Light. We must learn to flee our comfort zones and plunge headfirst into uncomfortable situations. That is where we can apply the most Resistance. True, the path of most Resistance causes some pain and discomfort for a moment, but it's the only way to generate long-term fulfillment. Difficult though it may seem, we should embrace rather than avoid problems and obstacles. They are the true opportunities and the quickest path to transformation, growth, and the ultimate in happiness.

The Million-Dollar Opportunity

We have been programmed to avoid problems and despise obstacles. We have been conditioned to refute and rebut every opinion and argument put forth by our enemies and friends alike.

Suppose you are in severe financial difficulty. God comes to you and says He will give you one million dollars every time someone hurts you or angers you—provided you completely *let go* of any reactive feelings. Simply put, you cannot take anything personally.

What would be on your mind all day?

You'd be praying for God to send you people to hurt you! You'd wake up every morning searching out all the difficult relationships, offensive people, and chaotic circumstances.

The Law of *Tikun*

In common with Eastern spiritual traditions, Kabbalah teaches that each of us comes to this world with baggage from previous life-times. This baggage contains all the situations where we short-circuited in our last lives, or at some forgotten point in this life. Each time we fail to resist our reactive behavior, we have to correct it at some point in the future. This concept of correction is called *Tikun*. We can have a *Tikun* with money, people, health, friendship, or relationships. There's an easy way to identify our personal *Tikun*. Whatever is painfully uncomfortable for us is part of our *Tikun*.

All the people in our lives who truly bother and annoy us, they too are part of our *Tikun*. If we find it difficult to say no to a salesperson calling on the phone during dinner hour, that is our *Tikun* and it needs to be corrected. If we are embarrassed about asking for a discount from a haughty salesclerk in an upscale designer's shop, you can be sure that is our personal *Tikun* and area of correction. If we find it difficult to confront an employee or an employer, the root cause is found within the concept of *Tikun*.

When we fail to make a correction by resisting our reactive behavior, it becomes more difficult to correct next time around in that specific area. That particular reactive trait grows stronger. Our Opponent grows stronger. Not only do we have to face the problem again, but it will be that much harder emotionally to activate Resistance. And next time around does not necessarily mean next life; these same corrections can appear over and over again in our present incarnations.

Sometimes it's a little too easy to blame past-life behavior for the problems in this life. We usually do enough rotten reactive stuff right here to warrant the chaos that afflicts us. This is the underlying reason why the same problems keep recurring. They may very well manifest through different people years later, but it's the same underlying problem again and again.

Seeking comfort and avoiding our *Tikun* produces momentary gratification and relief, but it is linked to long-term chaos. In contrast, *the bigger the obstacle, the greater the potential Light.*

With this new understanding, we can no longer be victims. We can no longer lament the hardships, problems, and uncomfortable circumstances that confront us, no matter how good that might feel, because all those difficulties are there to call down the everlasting Light of fulfillment into our lives. But first, there is a *Tikun* situation demanding to be corrected.

Groundhog Day

If you haven't seen the film *Groundhog Day*, go out and rent the DVD the moment you close this book. It's a wonderful demonstration of the Kabbalistic principle of *Tikun* in action.

In the film, Bill Murray plays Phil Connors, a TV weatherman/reporter and the ultimate reactive character. Here's a brief lowdown on the film:

> *Phil Connors is consumed in his own self-indulgence, conceit, and indifference to the world around him. One day, he gets stuck in a time warp in a small town in Pennsylvania. While covering a civic ceremony commemorating Groundhog Day, he is trapped inside the date of February 2.*
>
> *The same day keeps repeating itself over and over again and no one knows this but Phil. It's wildly fun at first, as Phil takes advantage of the situation, learning all he can about his world and the people in it in order to manipulate them and serve his own self-interests. He has a joyous time using and abusing everyone as he relives the same day every day. But his world slowly turns into a nightmare as the momentary pleasures wear off. He has exhausted all of the various scenarios of self-indulgence, and now there is not a drop of fulfillment to be found.*
>
> *Pushed to the point of suicide, he still awakes in the morning to find himself imprisoned in the same town confronting the same events. There is no escape—not even death. Finally, after enduring tremendous suffering, he decides to change himself because he cannot change*

the world around him. He begins to perform a few good deeds and help the people who are experiencing the same misfortunes each day.

Suddenly, he feels true fulfillment. Inspired by this Light, he goes on a rampage of sharing all over the town, gradually winning the hearts of everyone. Eventually he winds up with the girl of his dreams, and the nightmare has ended. He has broken the recurring cycle and finds himself in a brand-new day, arm in arm with his true soul mate. His prison has become paradise!

This is the law of *Tikun*, and this is the reason our lives sometimes feel like we're trapped in a bad movie.

Groundhog Life

At first, it's fun to indulge in our reactive behavior. We take advantage of others, and everything we do, we do out of self-interest. But *payback* eventually rears its ugly head and that's when we find ourselves mired in serious chaos and pain. The same problems recur day after day and still we do not learn our lessons. We fail to connect our reactions to our chaos.

But then, when we are finally pushed to the point of unbearable suffering after enduring this awful nightmare cycle year after year, lifetime after lifetime, we begin to wake up. We come across a book on Kabbalah and we realize that *stopping* our reactions, overthrowing our ego, and caring more about the people around us than we do for our Opponent actually generates genuine Light in our lives. We've never really experienced this kind of lasting Light before because we've become so accustomed to the short-term highs and thrills of reactivity. But this *lasting Light* is different. It feels good. Really good. *So this is what genuine happiness feels like!*

Now we are motivated to transform all of our reactive impulses and live life in a proactive state. We find our soul mate and wind up forever living in the Light.

By the way, we don't have to reach the point of extreme suffering to wake up.

The moment you start learning Kabbalah, everything changes.

Resistance at Work

Here are some situations to help enhance your understanding of Resistance and the opportunities that lie within difficult circumstances that are part of a *Tikun*:

Resisting Ego

You're with a group of friends or business acquaintances. Everyone is talking, showing off their expertise about a particular topic, but it's obvious to you that you know much more than they do about the subject. You feel pressure to speak and flaunt your knowledge. Resist: It's your ego! Don't talk. Don't say a word. Recognize the spiritual opportunity and let it go. The Light will enter and you may learn something valuable from the conversation.

Resisting Inverted Ego

After a business presentation, everyone is asking questions except you. You feel pressured. Insecure. You're afraid of what the people in the room might be thinking about you. You become self-conscious. Your immediate reaction is to speak out of insecurity. This is *inverted* ego-thinking: You are not good enough. Resist! Let it go! Worrying about what others think is reactive behavior. Later, you'll probably have about a half dozen people approach you and strike up a conversation; you will see that your insecurity was totally unwarranted and no one even noticed.

Resisting Laziness

A great idea comes to you. You are totally excited about it and are intent upon acting upon it. Then procrastination sets in. You put it off. Resist this laziness! Resistance doesn't necessarily mean stopping and standing still. Often it means stopping the desire to stop and diving in head first. Here, your *Tikun* is about not being able to finish what you start.

Resisting Judgment

An argument erupts between your family members or close friends. You hear one side of the story and are appalled. You're ready to pass judgment and choose sides. Resist! Let go of your emotions. Listen and hear the other side. Your *Tikun* is probably connected to judgmental behavior. You will discover that there are two sides to this story—and to every story.

Here is a remarkable and profound universal law: According to Kabbalah, your own reactive actions, your own so-called sins, your own negative behavior, can never ever come back to judge you on its own. Your words and confessions can never inflict retribution upon you. The force we call God cannot judge you, either. The cosmos will never penalize you. This is a rock-solid Kabbalistic principle of life. Pretty incredible, isn't it?

How, then, do we invite so much judgment into our lives? Good question.

Kabbalah says the world is strategically arranged and set up so that all the people in our lives, from close friends to casual acquaintances, from our dearest family members to the strangers that pass us by in the street, all these folks share similar sins to our own. Here's what happens: The reactive negative traits of others will be shown to us during the course of our daily life. The moment we choose to pass judgment (rightly or wrongly) upon another individual, we have pulled the trigger on ourselves. Only the words we speak against others allow the Opponent to inflict payback upon us as a result of our own previous reactions. Only when we pass judgment on another person can the Opponent execute a guilty verdict upon us.

Conversely, if we apply Resistance and withhold judgment upon a person, then judgment can never befall us. Imagine those possibilities. What a kind, merciful, and forgiving world we could inhabit if we just stopped judging others by utilizing the tool of Resistance.

So make up your mind to Resist all your justified acts of judgments so you can protect yourself from your own nasty and dastardly reactive deeds.

Resisting Self-Involvement

You're confused over some important decisions, worried about their impact on your life. You deliberate, analyze, worry, fret, fuss, and stress out. Resist the urge to anguish over yourself! Go and do something good for someone else. Invest a little time helping others with their problems. When you get out of your own way, solutions will come to you when you least expect them.

Resisting Self-Praise

You did something really wonderful, and everyone admires you for it. You are now tempted to relive the glory and replay it over and over again in your mind. Resist these self-serving recollections! Think bigger. What else can you do? What's next? Move on to the next positive deed.

Resisting Evil Impulses

Things aren't going well. You're feeling a little down and a bit insecure about yourself. Suddenly, a friend calls. After a moment of small talk, the friend begins bad-mouthing another close friend. You get sucked into the conversation. Knocking down someone else makes you feel better about yourself. Hearing about someone else's problems makes you feel better about your own situation. Resist the desire to gossip and speak bad about others! Remember, Kabbalistically, the sin of murder is not limited to physical death; it includes character assassination. Terminating the conversation, or changing the subject, is therefore the equivalent of saving someone's life. This will reveal tremendous Light, which will truly help with your problems.

Resisting Control

You're a new writer who's just completed what you believe is a great manuscript. You show it to a friend who happens to be an editor. You're expecting high praise, but your friend criticizes it. You take the hard-hitting critique personally and begin losing your confidence. *Resist!* Your reaction means you believe you're the true source of this material, not the Light. True artists know they are just a channel. Moreover, even the *criticism* comes from the Light. So give up control. Trust the process and let go of your personal attachment to the work.

Resisting Guilt

You did something wrong—really wrong—so you beat yourself up pretty badly. You lay the guilt on heavily. *Resist* the compulsion to self-destruct! Let it go. Embrace the Kabbalistic truth that there are two sides within each of us. Proactive and reactive. Light and darkness. The soul and the Opponent. The part that needs correction and transformation, and the God-aspect of ourselves that will help us transform. Don't ignore the wrongdoing, but look at it as an opportunity. Falling spiritually and picking ourselves back up again is how we create spiritual transformation.

Resisting Expectations

You are full of expectations for your work, but they fail to materialize. You expect certain responses from friends; they let you down. You have clear ideas about the way certain people should treat you after all that you've done for them; they prove to be ungrateful. You have expectations about a long-awaited holiday; it rains every day and someone steals your credit cards. Resist all your feelings of disappointment! Stop those feelings of victimization. Something better is coming. Embrace the Kabbalistic principle of asking the Light for what you need in life, *not for what you want.* Later, you will see the real blessing and spiritual reason for the disappointment.

A few years ago a good friend, whom I'll call Robert, told me that his brother had had a strange dream. In his dream, Robert's brother saw himself without any clothes on. Kabbalistically, this image can be interpreted as a negative sign.

Robert told his brother to purchase a set of the holy Zohar, which is said to bring blessing and protection to the individual. Robert's brother was skeptical, so Robert bought the set for him. Surprisingly, his brother accepted the gift.

A few days later, Robert's brother was rushing to the airport to catch a plane to Paris. The airport was mobbed. At that moment, fighting through the crowds, Robert's brother wanted more than anything to make his flight because he had to be in Paris on business. Nevertheless, he missed the plane. And he was awfully upset about it at the time—especially when he found out that all his luggage was *already* on board.

The flight that Robert's brother missed was TWA Flight 800 to Paris that crashed moments after it left Kennedy Airport on July 17, 1996. All 230 people on board perished in this terrible tragedy. Missing the plane was not what Robert's brother originally wanted. This is a dramatic example of how Light brings us what we truly need and not necessarily what we might want. There is *always* a bigger picture.

Resisting a Lack of Confidence

You have to speak in public, or take responsibility for a major project. Your natural reaction might be, "I can't do it, I'm not good enough, I don't want all the attention focused upon me." This is reversed ego. Let go of your limited thinking. It's not even about you. There's a bigger picture that includes other people, not just yourself. Focus on finding a way to help them get what they need and you'll find yourself succeeding effortlessly.

Resisting Selfishness

You arrive home from a bustling day at work. An important business deal consumes your mind. Your children want your attention, but you are too preoccupied calculating all the facts and figures. You'll play with them another time—after all, you tell yourself, you are doing all this for your family. Rubbish! *Resist* those fanciful, self-serving reactions. This is really all about you. The thrill of the deal. The profit and power. These are common selfish desires. Give your kids your time when it's the most difficult.

The following is a true story, told by a longtime student of Kabbalah:

> *I was the typical ambitious person who focused all his time and efforts on making money. Naturally, I thought I was doing everything for my wife and children. I began studying Kabbalah and I learned that there are two kinds of fulfillment. There is the short-term pleasure of gratifying one's own ego, and then there's fulfillment that's everlasting. Everlasting fulfillment is achieved when our efforts are proactive and for the sake of sharing with others. Ninety-five percent of us are all desperately trying to seek fulfillment for the sake of our own desire—to fulfill our own selfish needs. I understood this Kabbalistic principle intellectually but I never internalized it, never lived it—until I found myself in deep financial trouble.*

> *I was living in my ultimate dream home in Los Angeles when suddenly my business started collapsing. I though, This is the spiritual path? I'm supposed to have everything. What's happening? But I still didn't understand what "everything" really meant. So in this very pressured time in our lives, in order to alleviate some of the stress, my wife and I decided to watch the Academy Awards. I had never missed the Oscars since I was a kid. I always had this dream that one day I would be up on that stage with an*

acceptance speech for Best Picture of the Year.

Money was severely tight, but my wife and I decided to splurge and bought some take-out food that we couldn't really afford, just to give ourselves a break from the chaos. By the time we settled in front of the TV, the preshow was already rolling. It was pure relief to escape into that world for a while.

Now, I've got four kids, and my oldest son, David, who was nine years old at the time, came over to me and said, "Dad? Is this show more important than me?" Thank God for Kabbalah because right away, I knew this was a test for me, an opportunity, so I said, "Of course not." And so David said, "Well, then will you play with me instead?"

I have to admit, with some shame, I was torn. Really torn. I wanted to watch the Oscars. I didn't feel like playing. But I learned in Kabbalah that one must do what one doesn't want to do when it comes to giving of oneself. In other words, when it's difficult to do, Resist and do it anyway. That's when it is considered real sharing and proactive behavior. Most parents will play with their kids when they are in the mood. But how many of us really extend ourselves when we are totally not into it, for whatever good reason? When it's easy to play with our children, it is not real sharing, according to Kabbalah.

We must resist our selfish tendencies and go outside ourselves. At that moment in my life, the hard thing was to go play, and I was even ashamed to admit it to myself, because I wanted to watch the show so badly. So David and I went to play. We tossed the football back and forth, and I was thinking, All right, let's get this over with already.

I want to go back and watch. I'll do this for ten minutes and then I'll have done my duty as a father.

But I could feel this conflict brewing in my own mind. Then, David said to me, "Dad, are you going to go back and watch?"

I said, "Why?"

"Because I'd like you to play with me 'til bedtime."

That meant no Academy Awards. But I knew right then and there that I was being tested. That's when I really did Resistance. I thought, Okay, let it go. I'm not watching the stupid show. I am going to really play with my son!

Kabbalah taught me that when I play with my children, I must truly enter into their world, not just put in time with them. So I got into it. It wasn't easy at first. It was a struggle to break away from my selfish desires and thoughts. But when I realized what was happening, I found the strength to resist and let it all go. And then we really started playing, tossing the ball, having some serious fun together. It was amazing. Then all of a sudden, my son burst into tears. He was crying his eyes out. I asked, "What's the matter?"

And he said, "I don't know. I just feel so happy." Tears were literally streaming down his cheeks.

And that's how it happened. That's when I realized what a selfish father I had been for years. I was under the delusion that buying this big house, accumulating material wealth, was for my wife and children. It wasn't. It was for me. They didn't want such a massive house and all the "extra" money. All my children wanted was a game of football with their Dad, along with his undivided love and attention. And I was obsessed about watching the Academy Awards, and winning an Oscar one day, and achieving great success in business. I was the epitome of a person's selfish, self-seeking, egocentric desires.

The pleasure I was getting from gratifying my own ego wasn't nearly as rewarding and as amazing as hearing my child say he is so happy because of the joy I brought to him. So it was this huge awakening.

I learned something else: Our nature, by design, prevents us from really feeling the true fulfillment life can offer us. We get tempted by momentary and instant gratification of material success, anything that immediately satisfies the ego. And because it is easier to connect to immediate gratification than it is to true fulfillment, which requires effort and internal change, we naturally gravitate toward instant material happiness.

There are actual blockages where you become desensitized to the genuine fulfillment that life can offer you. When you apply Resistance, the shell breaks apart, the blockages are removed, and you start living. You begin feeling what true happiness is. When you let go, you start living so fully that your egocentric needs don't even become an issue anymore. The real fulfillment is there. You strike that elusive balance between business, family, and sharing. You give of yourself because it's the most natural thing in the world to do so. And then you have it all.

That night, I had begun to learn how to be a real father to my children.

It's also important not to get down on yourself and think you're a lousy parent when it's hard to focus during play. Resist that as well. The fact that you are conscious of what's happening, and making the effort, will bring Light to the situation. Recognize that the Opponent is playing mind games with you. He's behind the whole thing—all your dreams of power and wealth. When the Opponent is pulling your strings, no matter how high you climb, he will make you feel like it's never enough. In your relentless and futile pursuit, your family will slip away. Resistance will prevent that from happening.

Contrary to what the evil aliens tell us in all those *Star Trek* flicks, resistance is *not* futile. *Resistance is fulfillment!* The true Light that comes from family is often hard to reveal and experience. The Opponent can make the thrill of business feel better than the comforts of home—on the surface level—until it's too late. When, however, you apply the concept of Resistance, suddenly you will find a sense of contentment and joy you never knew before.

Resisting Insecurity

You and a partner worked long and hard on a project. It's a smashing success. Now you're afraid of sharing too much credit. You try to calculate who did what, out of your own insecurity. It will hurt your ego if everyone thinks your partner was the major contributor to the project. *Resist* those reactive thoughts and feelings! Then give away all the credit. That's right. Give it way. Everything. Let go completely. As you are about to do this, you may think, I should only resist a little bit, not too much, because I have to practice all this Kabbalah stuff one step at a time. Balderdash! *Resist these thoughts as well,* and give *all* the credit to your partner. Remember, the Opponent will test you every step of the way. Remember, praise gives pleasure for a moment; Light remains eternal. Don't trade away the farm for a bit of ego gratification.

Resisting Embarrassment

You make a big mistake. If everyone notices, you'll turn purple and die of embarrassment. You react and try to cover it up. *Resist!* Love the humiliation. Take it all in. Lower your defenses. Lower your guard. Walk through the mishap slowly and soak up as much embarrassment as possible. Make yourself vulnerable. Recognize that this is an opportunity to wipe out your ego. In the end, your ego will be subjugated, and you will see that no one even noticed your error. That's how the Light works.

Resisting the Need to Be Admired

You're out with friends and you're meeting new acquaintances. You're introduced by your friends as the smart one in your group. Now you feel pressure to respond to a difficult question, and you're not 100 percent sure of the answer. Your initial reaction is to fake it and ramble through as best as you can. Resist! Just say, "I don't know." Leave it at that. Then resist those reactive thoughts that tell you that your friends might not like, admire, or look up to you anymore.

Resisting Doubts

You apply the wisdom of Kabbalah in your life. You use the principle of Resistance in a real-life situation. There are no results. Doubts flood your mind. It doesn't work, you say to yourself. *Resist* these reactive thoughts! It's a test to see if you've truly surrendered. The Opponent is merely delaying the Light. Whenever you look for results, you've blown the entire exercise. That's the ultimate paradox. Look for results and they won't come. Give it up, and you'll get it all!

• • •

That's about all this book can do for you on this particular topic. The rest is up to you. You have to jump into the chaotic situations of life and "just do it." You will know the power and magic of Resistance when you experience it in real life.

But guess what?

Once you've switched from reactive to proactive, you've removed Bread of Shame. You've spiritually transformed yourself in that situation. You are now ready and able to receive the everlasting Light of fulfillment in that part of your life. You have accomplished the purpose of your existence in that specific circumstance.

However, the Opponent has one more trick up his sleeve . . .

The Power of a Short Circuit

Recall a moment when a light bulb burst in your home. When it short-circuited, there was a momentary intense flash of light. *Then there was darkness.*

What happened?

The filament broke.

The positive pole connected directly into the negative pole.

Poof!

A short circuit.

A burst of light.

Darkness.

Did you notice how the spark of light generated by a short circuit is always far stronger and brighter than the light of the bulb when it was burning normally? Spiritual Light works the same way.

Momentary pleasure invoked by reactive behavior is much more powerful and intoxicating than the ongoing pleasure of Light that is generated by Resistance. But a reactive burst of pleasure will always be followed by darkness.

These are the laws of electrical current. These are the laws of spiritual current.

Temptation

Our Opponent flashes immense pleasure in front of our five senses at every opportunity. All too often we accept his offer, because reactive behavior is very tempting. It delivers an overwhelming burst of energy.

The *intensity* of resisted Light may not be as brilliant as the flash of a short circuit, but the *volume* of illumination produced by Resistance is far greater.

Drugs and alcohol similarly demonstrate the power of a short circuit. According to Kabbalah, intoxicants do elevate the soul to higher levels of the spiritual atmosphere. As psychoanalyst Carl Jung pointed out, it is not by accident that alcohol is also called spirits. The problem is, drugs connect us very directly to these energy forces. As a result, we short-circuit. We crash. We burn, and then we burn out.

There is an important distinction between moralistic reasons for abstaining from drugs versus the Kabbalistic viewpoint. While it *is* our purpose in life to ascend to higher states of consciousness, drugs and alcohol are completely inadequate to fulfill this intention. We need to find ways of achieving that higher state of existence permanently rather than momentarily. But the Opponent constantly uses the power of instant gratification and momentary highs to ignite our reactions. His sole purpose is to create short circuits directly so that we will eventually plunge ourselves into darkness.

Crash Diet

Barbara is 30 pounds overweight. She has been dieting and exercising for a couple of weeks. But then someone kindly offers her a piece of chocolate cake, her favorite. The reactive instinct of her body is to thankfully accept. But a conflict brews in Barbara's mind: Should she give up the diet for now and start again on Monday, or stick with the program?

Barbara attempts to arouse her willpower. She summons as much strength as she can while she tries to remember the passion behind her initial pledge to lose weight. She desperately wants to find that original sense of dedication toward a healthier lifestyle. Yes, she wants to fit into her old jeans again! Barbara wants to hold true to her goal of losing the weight. She knows she must resist.

Suddenly, someone else is on the scene. The Opponent fills Barbara's mind with desires that are richly vivid and compelling, and Barbara is slowly breaking down at the thought of licking creamy fudge off a fork. She finally succumbs to the reactive urge.

Once she has surrendered control, she might as well eat the cake for all it's worth. At least, that's what the Opponent tells her. And she does eat it. And it tastes wonderful. Soon Barbara's body is enjoying a sugar rush. And the cannabinoids in the chocolate are inducing the same kind of high that marijuana delivers. And the chocolate acts as a cheap substitute for love because it contains a stimulating substance that generates the rush we feel when we fall in love. The cocoa fat is prompting the production of opiates in Barbara's brain, which arouse further feelings of pleasure. And then there is that old favorite, caffeine, which is stimulating her brain and pumping adrenaline through her veins. Instant gratification!

But the story is not over yet. Suddenly, the rush of pleasure wears off. Barbara's blood sugar plummets. She crashes. Kabbalistically, the Light from the cake has been cut off in a short circuit. Barbara is now overwhelmed by all-too-familiar feelings of guilt, regret, depression, and disappointment.

If Barbara had resisted her reactive desire to consume the cake and had eaten an apple instead, her body and soul would have felt satiated. Not in an intense way, but in a tempered, balanced, and fulfilling way. More important, 24 hours later, feelings of accomplishment, self-worth, and fulfillment would have stayed with her.

We face tough decisions every day in business, social situations, and family life. Do we continue reacting to all the external stimuli coming from every direction? Or do we stop the reactions in order to bring a bit of spiritual sanity into our lives?

For some reason, it's just not easy to resist immediate gratification. We set our minds toward the goal of not reacting, but when the time comes, we're ambushed by the fleeting pleasures of a reactive moment. As we read these ideas in this book, we get excited for the moment. The next day, someone insults us, a business deal falls through, someone speaks badly of us, and we fall back into our reactive ways.

Before we discover why we have such difficulty resisting temptation, we must reveal another weapon in the Opponent's arsenal.

The Faustian Pact

Whenever things start going really well, we may fall into the trap of believing that good times will never end. We become arrogant. We believe we are infallible.

Kabbalah teaches us that Light comes from two sources—the Creator and the Opponent. Remember, the Light of the Creator is an eternal flame. The Light of the Opponent is the bright flash from a stick of dynamite. When we strive for success with reactive behavior, our success comes from the Opponent. The more reactive we are, the more success we generate—at a price!

According to Kabbalah, the Faustian myth of selling one's soul to the Devil is very close to the truth.

The Faustian principle is at work almost every day: Be reactive and the Opponent will give you Light, albeit temporarily. When that Light is taken away, the Opponent gets to keep the real Light of the Creator. You get to keep the chaos after the dynamite blows.

Kabbalah teaches us that the Opponent will pay us well for a while just to keep us in a reactive state of mind. In other words, he simply gives us a stick of dynamite with an extra-long fuse (time) so that the illusion of success and Light lasts longer.

When we are flying high, we believe that we are the brilliant orchestrators of our own success. Our egos are inflated to the size of the Goodyear blimp, and just as full of hot air. And when we least expect it, they deflate.

Slavery

Most everyone is familiar with the biblical story of the Exodus. But most people, including most rabbis and priests, don't recognize the hidden spiritual significance of this story and its clear importance in our own lives.

The story tells us that the Israelites were in bondage in Egypt for 400 years. They were slaves and the children of slaves, held captive to the hardhearted Pharaoh, ruler of Egypt. There came a great leader by the name of Moses, who, on a mission from God, won the freedom of his people. Moses then led the former slaves on a long and arduous journey, which included that famous detour through the Red Sea, and on to Mount Sinai for a date with destiny.

But here's the interesting part. The Israelites were tasting freedom for the first time in centuries, yet they still managed to complain, whine, and grumble the moment it got a little hot and sticky in the desert. They actually begged Moses to take them back to Egypt!

According to Kabbalah, this entire story is a code. *Egypt* is a code word for our material existence in this physical world of chaos. *Pharaoh* is a code for the human ego and humanity's incessantly reactive, self-seeking, intolerant nature. Any aspect of our nature that controls us is Pharaoh.

- Fear

- Anger

- Competitiveness

- Insecurity

- Low Self-Esteem

- Selfishness

- Envy

- Anxiety

- Impatience

All these emotions, born of ego, constantly control and imprison us. They are like a ball and chain that slow us down and prevent us from moving forward. They are like handcuffs that constrain us; iron bars that trap us; whips that torment us. This is the oldest master-slave relationship in Creation. And it takes many forms:

We're imprisoned by the ego-based aspects of our material existence—cars, clothes, luxury homes, prestige, power, and position.

We're held in bondage by our reactive whims and ego-centric desires.

We're held captive by our careers, relationships, fears, and doubts.

We're prisoners to other people's perceptions of us.

We're incarcerated by our own desperate need for other people's acceptance.

We're hostages to a constant need to outdo and one-up

our friends and colleagues.

Some of us are trapped in our jobs.

Others are bound and gagged inside our marriages.

All of us are enslaved to the physical world around us.

But through awareness that we are still imprisoned in *Egypt*, enslaved to our ego, we can grasp the key that unlocks the chains and attain the greatest freedom people can know. This is the true power of Kabbalah.

The Power of Certainty

Fleeing the Egyptians, the Israelites were cornered on the banks of the Red Sea. Pharaoh and his army raced toward them, bent on their total annihilation. Suddenly the Red Sea parted, producing two massive walls of water that reached to the sky. According to the Zohar, all the waters of the earth split and rose toward the heavens. And the Israelites raced off to freedom.

When Pharaoh and his army were approaching, Moses had cried out to God for help. The Zohar teaches that God replied with a mysterious question: "Why are you calling to me?" Concealed within this question is a profound spiritual truth. God did not part the Red Sea! In fact, God was surprised that Moses even called upon Him at that moment. But if the almighty Creator did not part the waters, who did?

Many thousands of years later, another crisis took place. It was not a life-or-death situation, but it definitely seemed like one at the time. Although the names have been changed, this story is true.

Michael owned a direct-sales organization with offices across North America. After one of the best fourth-quarter sales periods in his company's history, Michael headed off to Miami with his wife and children for a ten-day holiday.

On his first day back, Michael's accountant walked into his office. With obvious discomfort, the accountant explained that one of the company's sales managers had sent in phony deposit slips for his sales during the last three weeks of December. The money had never made it into the company's bank account. Worse, this was their best manager, with the best-performing office in the organization.

"How much is missing?" Michael asked.

His accountant swallowed hard and told him, "The manager stole $105,000."

Michael poured himself a glass of water and took a small sip. As Michael remembers it: "At that moment I had a serious choice to make, and I had to make it fast. I could practice what I learned in my Kabbalah classes, or I throw it all out the window because of the large amount of money that was at stake. It was up to me."

A great deal of time had passed between the parting of the Red Sea and Michael's loss of more than $100,000. But it was knowledge of Kabbalah that enabled both the ancient Israelites and a contemporary suburbanite to discover startling solutions to their predicaments.

The Certainty Principle

At that moment, Michael had a decision to make. Should he react with fear, panic, and anger? Or should he call upon what he'd learned in his studies of Kabbalah—including the hidden lesson of the Red Sea's parting—and choose a proactive alternative?

Here's what Michael had learned regarding the dire straits of the Israelites as they stood on the brink of destruction. The Israelites did escape. And, yes, the Red Sea (and all the waters of the earth) did part magnificently. *But God didn't do it.* When God asked Moses why he was calling upon Him, God was implying that Moses and the Israelites had the power to part the Red Sea on their own. God was revealing one of the Spiritual Laws of Life: *Overcome your own reactive nature and the heavens will respond and help you overcome the laws of Mother Nature, for the two are intimately connected.*

Doing that requires total *certainty*. That is the secret interpretation of this story. The Israelites were forced to step into the waters of the sea and proceed with total certainty before a drop of water began to split. They were required to resist the overwhelming uncertainty that was ingrained into their natures.

In fact, Kabbalistic sages explained that the Red Sea did not part until the waters had reached the nostrils of the Israelites. And then, when the waters rushed into their throats, the Israelites relinquished control and demonstrated certainty in a positive outcome. They put their lives into the hands of the Light. A split second later, they were breathing fresh air as the waters parted and rose toward the heavens.

Michael was also on the verge of drowning. He looked at his

accountant and said, "The manager never stole the money. The money is not missing."

Then he added, "You can never lose something that is really yours. Therefore, the money has to show up. If it doesn't, it was never mine to begin with."

Michael was injecting proactivity into the situation. He would not react to *either* outcome. That was the key. He was certain that, whatever the outcome, it would be best for his spiritual understanding and growth.

His accountant was also certain—he was sure that Michael had gone off the deep end!

"Do I just stand here and do nothing?" the accountant cried. "Shouldn't we call the police and start an investigation? We are trying to run a company here!"

The accountant was completely locked into his belief that the money had been stolen. It took Michael an hour to convince him to be even slightly open to another possibility.

"First," Michael said, "I want you to accept the possibility that the money is not missing. Second, if it is missing, it was never ours. We would have lost it in another deal, or our profits would be lower next year by the same amount because our sales would fall. In other words, have the certainty that whatever happens, it is correct. We must have certainty that the outcome will be the best from a spiritual perspective. Once you have that state of mind, then continue on and do what you would normally do in this situation."

Although the accountant did not fully understand what Michael was talking about, he did come back the next morning with the news that $88,000 had suddenly turned up in a bank in Winnipeg, Manitoba, Canada.

"We found the checks," the accountant explained. The manager could not cash them so he deposited the checks and kept all the cash.

"No," Michael replied, "the manager did not steal the cash. The cash will also turn up. No one can take what is rightfully ours. And if it doesn't show up, it was not ours to begin with."

Michael was again making a proactive attempt not to be a slave, or to be under the control of any outcome, positive or negative. As it turned out, the manager had indeed intended to steal the money. But by the time he reached Florida, a couple of days later, he had a change of heart. He actually called Michael on the phone and confessed.

"There's no doubt in my mind my that the Kabbalistic concept of certainty played a major role in what happened," Michael said later. "Before I learned Kabbalah, I would have sent two guys with baseball bats to hunt the thief down. They probably would have never found him, and I'd still be out over $100,000. My blood pressure would have skyrocketed throughout this whole sordid affair and I'd be living a life filled with feelings of revenge, victimization, and negativity. Thankfully, I'm free of all that."

According to many spiritual teachings, Kabbalah included, consciousness creates our reality. What we desire is what we receive. If we are uncertain, we receive the energy of uncertainty. If we respond to crises with worry and negative thinking, we increase the likelihood of a painful outcome.

But it could all be very different. We can put an end to our uncertainty and doubt. We can disrupt the Opponent's agenda. By offering Resistance, we create a space for the Light to fill.

Miracle Making

If you want to see real miracles occur, try shutting down thoughts of uncertainty about positive outcomes when seemingly insurmountable obstacles confront you. Start focusing on removing Bread of Shame and shift your focus away from results and outcomes. Remember, *we already had the results in the Endless World*. Michael already had the joy that comes from $100,000 cash in your pocket. What Michael did *not* have in the Endless World was the ability to be proactive and unleash his God gene. He gained this opportunity in this world when the money departed and he did not react.

Once Michael seized this opportunity to remove Bread of Shame and transform from reactive to proactive, *he accomplished the original objective of the Vessel: to become the cause of his own fulfillment as opposed to being a reactive effect; to create something new—a proactive consciousness instead of reactive one.*

Once this feat was achieved, the Light was allowed to flow freely. The money was free to return because the purpose of creation was achieved. If Michael had reacted, he would have missed the opportunity and the money would have vanished for good. Worse, he would have been forced to confront a similar challenge (opportunity) again at some point in the future, because there was still a *Tikun*, a transformation waiting to take place.

To help maintain a proactive state of mind in difficult situations, we have the Eleventh Kabbalistic Principle:

When Challenges Appear Overwhelming, Inject Certainty. The Light Is Always There!

Injecting certainty into a situation does not mean we always get the result we want. Rather, certainty means knowing the Light's unseen hand is in the game with us. There may be times when we are behind on the scoreboard, but ultimately we can't lose.

Kabbalah teaches that the adversity in any situation is the truly positive element. Just as the antidote to a poisonous snakebite is contained in the venom, the Light is contained within the obstacles of life.

When we understand this principle, we enthusiastically embrace life's difficulties. We recognize them as opportunities to stop our instinctive reactions and to become true Creators in our lives.

Remember, certainty does not mean that we get what we want, but rather we get what we *need* in our lives to further our transformation and finally win this game of life. It's having certainty in *whatever* outcome is placed before us. It's having certainty that our reaction is what is important and nothing else. Not results. Not outcomes. It's accepting responsibility for the negativity that strikes in our lives. It's recognizing that the rotten stuff in our face is because we've planted a negative seed at some point in our past. When we overcome our uncertainty, we create miracles in our lives.

part five
how to win the game of life

The Art of Becoming God

Thus far, we have learned that in the Endless World every conceivable form of fulfillment existed. This includes the fulfillment we receive from music, art, architecture, money, movies, games, business, stories, eating, and every other human endeavor. But all this fulfillment was originally given to us for free. Gratis. Complimentary. *On the house.*

The God gene in our soul impelled us to want to become creators of our own fulfillment.

This is the underlying reason why in our world:

Writers love to write.

Singers love to sing.

Inventors love to invent.

Scientists love to discover.

Architects love to design.

Builders love to build.

Tailors love to sew.

Businessmen love to make deals.

Musicians love to compose.

These are all expressions of a human being becoming like the

Creator. All the inventions, songs, poems, stories, discoveries, and infinite wisdom of life were already contained in the Endless World. But we said, *Hide it!*

So all the Light was veiled behind a curtain. Now we search for it again, in our own lives. When we rediscover it, we express the spark of godliness in our soul. The purpose of life is achieved in that one moment. But as we have discovered, there is a big *if!*

If we fall under the *very real illusion* that we, ourselves, are the sole creators of our success; *if* we achieve all these forms of fulfillment through our ego (face it, we do this 99.999 percent of the time) then all the true Light we've created *goes to the Opponent.*

Sure, we get a quick shot of pleasure that intoxicates our ego, but then we are left in the dark. And our Opponent is now that much stronger! We wind up strung out on coke, stricken with anxiety, or plagued with chronic insecurity. Our achievements are never enough. We still feel empty. Or we become lousy parents and our relationship with our kids is rotten. Or we become abysmal spouses and our marriages fall apart or become passionless and tiresome.

Somewhere along the line a price is paid for our pleasure. Success comes with side effects. Contentment comes at a cost.

When we conquer our ego and stop all reactions, we become proactive, just like God, and success and joy are now earned, unconditionally!

This is how the game of life operates.

Questions about This Game

Countless centuries have passed and it seems that the Opponent continues his winning streak, season after season. Uncertainty and doubt have been plagues throughout the millennia. The world has constantly been focused on results, not reactions, in the pursuit of happiness. Accordingly, instead of living in Light the world has floundered in darkness.

What does Kabbalah—and the Zohar in particular—have to say about how this game of life finally ends? Keep in mind, when the game of life is over, it does not mean the end of civilization. It means the end of death, pain, and suffering. It's the demise of the Opponent. It means humanity achieves world peace and permanent existence, beyond what we can imagine or conceive.

And finally, how do we apply all of the Kabbalistic principles learned thus far to the world at large?

The Final Innings

*I never give them hell. I just tell the truth
and they think it is hell.*
— Harry S. Truman

According to the ancient Kabbalists, the Hebrew Calendar Year of 5760 will mark an unprecedented new era of human existence. The Zohar describes this new era with two words—*woe and blessed.*

This specific date corresponds to the year 2001 in our Western Calendar.

Woe refers to a time of great upheaval, terror, and pain, affecting us both personally and globally. Throughout this era of torment, the egocentric nature of humans will be eradicated from our nature. The intense pressure will finally break the resolve of the ego, our Opponent,
and we will at last recognize the value and wisdom associated with treating others with nothing less than human dignity—be it our rival and colleague at work, or our enemy on the other side of the globe.

According to the Kabbalists, during this time of woe, our immune systems will come under attack. Diseases, new and old strains, will torment us. Globally, there will be wars, acts of terror, the destruction of the environment, the ruin of our drinking water, and other calamities involving and affecting Jews, Christians, Moslems, and all humanity.

Through these various global and personal tragedies, humanity will come to realize that the treasures procured through the ego are illusionary and fleeting, and come at a high cost.

We will finally pull together when the world around us is tragically ripped apart. We will at last realize the only real enemy out there is the Opponent, and not any one single human being.

The ancient Zohar offers precise passages relating to these times. These controversial statements describe actual and specific dates that will indicate to us that we have reached this period known as the *End of Days.*

End of Days

In volume 8 of the Zohar, paragraph 116, under a section appropriately entitled "The Coming of the Messiah," the Zohar speaks of the type of judgments that will strike the world's most powerful city to launch this new era in the year 2001:

"On this day, in the great tall city, there will be a flame of fire. The sound will awaken the entire world. It will burn many towers. Many towers will collapse and many prominent people and officers will fall on that day."

The ancient Kabbalists even calculated the exact Hebrew date from the Zohar as to when this might happen. The date given was the 23rd day of Elul. Well, in the year 5760 (2001), the 23rd day of Elul was September 11 in the Western calendar.

Furthermore, the prologue of the Zohar gives the actual name of a negative force that brings judgment into this world. This negative force is referred to by the metaphor of a dog:

"And because the Other Side saw this, it gained courage and sent a dog to eat the offerings. And what is the name of that dog? 'B' ladan' is its name . . . And He is not a human being."

While these Zohar statements are quite uncanny, I myself am not too fond of so-called spiritual prophecy or predictions for various Kabbalistic reasons, such as our ability to change and alter our destiny. Still, we have the most important book of Kabbalistic wisdom giving us an exact date, a precise name, and a fairly accurate description of the events of 9/11. It's easy to be skeptical. And it's just as easy to be dazzled. However, both of these responses are in the extreme. The fact is, the world is hurting right now. And the world has experienced a whole lot of hurt, pain, and suffering in *every* generation.

What *does* excite me about the Zohar is that it also tells us how to stop all the hurt and change our future for the better. Which leads us to the Zohar's explanation of *blessed*.

The Blessed

Blessed refers to a time of peace, tranquility, enlightenment, and eternal fulfillment. Disease will be decimated. Chaos will no longer exist. Joy will be everywhere. And the angel of death will be dead and buried.

Quite the opposite of woe. So what's the message?

Both destinies are possible. Both fates are options for us to choose via our free will.

How do we control our fate? How do we ensure that we find ourselves in the universe of blessed, as opposed to the universe of woe?

The game of life is going to end no matter what. We are going to achieve our ultimate destiny of happiness. Our only free will is to decide *how* we get there.

We can remove our internal Opponent through constant suffering. Or we can conquer our ego through proactive Kabbalistic practice and arrive at happiness in a positive way.

But there is one prerequisite:

As Above, So Below

Violence in the world is not aimless chaos. Disease is not a haphazard occurrence. Terrorism is not random madness. Earthquakes are not acts of God. All these negative phenomena are born within the darkness that is created when our collective reactive behavior disconnects us all from the 99 percent reality. Grasping this difficult truth is the *prerequisite* to effecting true change. But grasping it is not easy. Make no mistake.

Consider this: A man eats three pastrami sandwiches a day. His father and his grandfather both died of heart attacks, and high cholesterol runs in this person's family.

Yet this person lives a long, healthy life.

Here's the point: When a man is disconnected from the 99 percent, enslaved to the will of his ego, ruled by the anger and hostility born of rash behavior, he creates openings for sickness, be it financial, health, or material.

This, and nothing else, is the root cause of all illnesses and strife, for it causes darkness on the spiritual level, and bodily or emotional dysfunction on the physical level.

The foods we eat and the fights we fight are merely *effects* and not the ultimate causative factors behind our chaos. They are simply the weapons used by our Opponent to physically manifest the spiritual darkness caused by our insensitive, reactive behavior.

Remember what we learned in the opening chapters of this book: Physical creation came about when the collective souls of humanity *rejected* the endless Light of Fulfillment that was originally bestowed upon them by the Creator.

We did this in order to gain the opportunity to earn and create this fulfillment through our own effort. Moreover, just as an athlete requires competition to give meaning to the concept of victory, our Opponent was created to challenge us during this process.

Our Opponent will use time to delay the rewards of good behavior so that we believe, mistakenly, that goodness does not pay off. Our Opponent will use time to delay "payback" caused by reactive behavior so that we believe, erroneously, that life lacks true justice.

We can now use the wisdom of Kabbalah to expose this illusion and see the bigger picture.

The path to the final result of eternal world peace is ours to choose—self-indulgent egocentric living, or spiritual transformation—woe and blessed, respectively.

Here in the 21st century, both realities will exist side by side, according to the Zohar. The gray areas of life will vanish. A line will be drawn in the sand. Clear distinctions will be made. Those who embrace spiritual transformation—from reactive behavior to proactive—will dwell in a proactive bubble of serenity even though the world around them might exist in rubble and ruin.

This is the promise of Kabbalah.

The choice is ours. It always has been.

How to Create the World of Blessed

Listen to the inner voice that is on
the other side of your ego.
— Unknown

The circumstances of our lives and global conditions will depend upon the individual and collective, reactive and proactive actions of humankind.

The state of the world is merely the sum total of the interactions of humanity. Black holes in space, tornadoes in Oklahoma, sunny days, calm seas, peace among nations, available parking spaces—everything rides on the interactions between one human being and another.

When the ancient sages declared that the earth is the center of the universe, they were not speaking about physical coordinates, They were speaking in spiritual terms. Our spiritual actions, be they reactive or proactive deeds, drive the cosmos.

From our dearest friends to our worst enemies, we are all connected on a deeper level of reality.

When the accumulated intolerant actions of humans can become so great, they create a mass of negativity that literally blocks the Light of the 99 percent from flowing into our 1 percent world, this is how chaos is born.

The simple, reactive act of yelling at your friend, speaking abusively to your spouse, or cheating someone in business tilts your life and the entire world to the side of woe.

By the same token, each act of Resistance, when you reel in your ego by admitting your jealousies to those you envy, or you give up your long-held, brilliant opinions for the sake of unifying with an opposing party, or you resist the urge to gain honor and prestige for yourself, tilts your existence—*and all existence*—toward the side of blessed.

The Opponent Strikes Back

Guess what? Your Opponent *knows* the impact your individual transformation has upon your life and the world. So he will constantly try to talk you out of this spiritual truth. He will try to make you reject this entire idea by using your rational mind. He would rather sell you products like "chance," "randomness," "accidental," and his favorite matching set, "lucky and unlucky."

- *Life is not that simple,* he will tell you.

- *As individuals we have no control over the world,* so he says.

- *My simple kindness to a stranger has no effect on reducing terrorism,* he will claim.

Well, life *is* that simple, according to Kabbalah.

And that's when he will try to convince you of the biggest falsehood of them all:

It is better to intellectualize, philosophize, politicize, and militarize all the events of our life and this world when seeking solutions. Forget spirituality. Forget Kabbalah. Forget accountability. Let's keep on doing the same things we've been doing, and thus, keep the fires burning!

If, however, we resist those dead-end, self-destructive notions and we embrace proactive transformation and kindness as the way to change our lives *and the world,* we wind up in a personal universe of blessed. As this transformation revolution of Kabbalah increases in the world, a critical mass will be achieved, and the chaos of life will vanish forever like a long-forgotten dream.

In fact, the Zohar says quite emphatically that those who embrace the Zohar, those who treasure it, study it, live it, and meditate upon it, *even if they don't understand a singe world,* for these people the Zohar becomes:

- A TREE OF LIFE

- A NOAH'S ARK

- PROTECTION FROM DEATH

- A PATH OF TRANSFORMATION THAT IS KIND-HEARTED AS OPPOSED TO CRUEL

This is the absolute promise of the Zohar.

Which leads us directly back to the opening quote of this book:

In seeking Wisdom, the first stage is silence,
the second listening, the third remembrance,
the fourth practicing, the fifth teaching.

— Kabbalist Solomon Gabirol

Teaching Others

World peace begins with personal peace. Period. As we begin to experience the Light of Kabbalah, we must share it with others to gain the truly full benefit.

Teaching Kabbalah, however, does *not* mean preaching Kabbalah.

To teach means to be a living example, a model for others, a beacon of Light. The gentle radiance that we generate will automatically inspire others to this wisdom. To teach means to share this wisdom with others out of love and care, not because we want to convert someone. Or convince someone. Or sell to someone.

Perhaps the most powerful way to share this Light is through the Zohar itself.

The Zohar radiates Light, which eradicates darkness merely by its presence in our lives or in volatile regions throughout the world.

Over the last 70 years, the Zohar has stopped earthquakes. Redirected hurricanes. Averted fatal collisions. Prevented wars. Inspired leaders to change their way of thinking.

Over the years, a diverse collection of people have come into contact with the Zohar through my father Rav Berg. Jews. Arabs. Moslems. Christians. Kings. Heads of state. Business leaders. And regular people like you and me. I have seen how the power of the Zohar touched and transformed their lives. Some of these people were on the most extremely negative path you could imagine, yet they changed their lives.

I watched people who might otherwise be categorized as enemies embrace my father in tears, and ask for blessings. They opened up their hearts because they felt the Light of the Zohar and this wisdom, as have many influential people throughout history. (See "A Brief History of Kabbalah" following this chapter.)

It wasn't something intellectual that touched all these people. It wasn't a specific piece of wisdom or particular principle that caused two enemies to embrace in respect and love.

What was it then?

The Power of Light

The Zohar is a candle in a world of darkness. It transcends religion, race, politics, and geography.

The Zohar is not merely made of paper and ink. The Zohar is the greatest force of divine energy known to humanity. Historians are now realizing that the Zohar is the authentic Holy Grail. It's the actual *Tree of Life* spoken of by *all* religions.

The secret of the Zohar's unparalleled power is remarkably simple: The Zohar radiates the Light of the 99 percent. In the same way that a lit light bulb eradicates darkness from a room, the spiritual Light of the Zohar banishes all forms of darkness from our world, including disease, depression, discontent, and even death itself.

People often ask me, "Is the Zohar a book of religion?" The answer is no! Not at all! Does gravity affect only Christians? Do the rays of the sun shine only upon Muslims? Of course not!

The Zohar's spiritual power is universal. The Zohar bestows blessings and the power of miracles upon *all* those who desire its true Light. Its power is intended for Christians, Muslims, Hindus, Jews, and all humanity. After all, everyone is entitled to happiness and a fulfilling and productive life free of chaos.

A darkened auditorium must respond to the light of a single candle. But no matter how much more darkness one adds—say, by enlarging the auditorium—no amount of darkness can snuff out the Light. This is a very profound phenomenon. And it lies at the very heart of this book.

When you grasp this, you've grasped the ultimate secret of the Zohar and Kabbalah.

In Conclusion: Go and Learn

Trying to live our lives in a manner of complete accountability is perhaps the most difficult of all tasks. It is so much easier for us to take up causes, seek out new paths of wisdom, or try to change the world, instead of just looking inward and trying to change ourselves while knowing that we are helping to elevate the entire world when we do so.

Our Opponent will be there every step of the way, putting temptation in our path. He makes gossip tempting and delicious. It will feel so much better to find wrong in others than to look in the mirror and find those same wrongs in ourselves. It is easier to become an activist waging war against all the corruption *out there* instead of being an activist who battles to change all those hidden egocentric impulses concealed *within*.

According to Kabbalah, if there is poverty in the world, it means we still have a measure of greed in our own souls. If there is a murder committed anywhere in the world, it means we still speak unkind words when we lose our temper. If there is abuse and corruption in our own field of vision, either on TV or in person, it means there is still a part of us that enjoys the negative impulses of our ego, no matter how pure, righteous, and well-intentioned we believe we are.

However, our Opponent blinds us to our own faults. We find it extremely difficult to detect them, let alone admit to them. So, here is some advice from the mystics who mastered the secrets of our mysterious universe: No longer are we to consider ourselves victims. From this point onward, we must accept responsibility for the rotten stuff that happens in our lives. We must admit that we are the cause. We must realize that we alone, by way of our previous actions, knowingly or unknowingly, have invited situations and people into our lives that will illuminate and bring out all of our destructive traits that we came here to transform.

This represents a profound and dramatic shift in human consciousness. It goes against every inclination and natural tendency in our instinctive nature. It means that we are the creators of every chaotic moment in our lives. It means that we recognize ourselves as the cause of our own misfortune.

In case you've forgotten, being the cause is one of the main attributes of being proactive. And as we've learned throughout this book, becoming proactive is the ultimate purpose of our existence.

Thus, when we transcend past our inborn power of impulse; when we rise above the impelling force of animal instinct; when we stop pointing the finger of blame at someone else and, instead, clench a fist and strike a stunning blow to our real Opponent in the game of life, we will make contact with the 99 percent realm.

We will connect ourselves to an infinite, endless emanation of Light. We will have invoked the infinite power of God in our lives. And then the awesome power to change anything and everything will, at once, be placed in the palms of our hands.

The Mirror

Suppose there was a mirror that reflected all your negative character traits, all the reactive instincts you came to this world to transform. Now suppose you smashed the mirror and broke it into 1,000 little pieces. Each piece would reflect a different negative characteristic of your nature. Now suppose you scattered all those pieces all over the place.

Guess what? All the negative people in your life, all the negative situations and obstacles that you confront or witness on the evening news, all the things you see wrong in others, are merely additional pieces of that mirror. Each fragment represents a different reflection *of your own character.* When you fix and transform a particular piece of your character, a fragment of mirror will reflect this transformation. You will begin to see the positive aspects of other people. Situations will begin to change for the better. People will become nicer. More caring. More loving. More genuine. And, even more remarkable, the external world will change in very tangible ways. (When a critical mass of people live life in this Kabbalistic fashion, peace on earth and everlasting happiness will arrive in a flash.)

Remember that everything in your life is there for one reason and one reason only: to offer you the opportunity to transform. Transformation is the only way to effect positive change in your life and in this world. Stop wasting your energy finding fault in others. Start the transformation within. Start looking for the uncomfortable situations in life and avoiding the easy routes. The Light will be found only in the rough waters of life. Why? Because choppy seas trigger reactions.

Sure, it will be turbulent for a while. You'll be buffeted from all sides at first. But if you remain certain that you are only being tested and if you don't react, the seas will calm down quickly. And that's when you'll come to know the power of Kabbalah. That's when you'll experience an extraordinary Light that has been trying to reach you and give you everything you've ever desired since time began.

And so we come to the final and Twelfth Principle:

All of the Negative Traits That You Spot in Others Are Merely a Reflection of Your Own Negative Traits.

When All Is Said and Done

There is one additional insight for the game of life. This one secret embodies and embraces all the principles we have learned thus far.

If you have trouble remembering all the lessons laid out in this book, the Kabbalists gave us a unique bit of wisdom that contains all the other principles within it. It's like a magic secret and it is revealed to us by way of an old Kabbalistic parable that goes something like this:

> *A young student, eager to master all the secrets of Kabbalah, approaches his revered teacher and master. The student is lugging along a box containing 22 sacred volumes of Kabbalistic books. He lays the heavy box down with a thud in front of his master and pleads with him to teach him all of its sublime secrets and magnificent mysteries in the short time that it takes to remain balanced on one leg. This eminent Kabbalist is one of the greatest spiritual giants to ever walk this earth. Upon hearing his eager student's request, he considers the question very carefully. His eyes then sparkle with infinite wisdom . . . and he says:*

Love thy neighbor as thyself.

All the rest is mere commentary.

Now go and learn.

appendix

Kabbalah's 12 Rules of the Game

1. Don't believe a word you read. Test-drive the lessons learned.

2. Two basic realities exist: Our 1 percent world of darkness and the 99 percent realm of light!

3. Everything that a human being truly desires from life is spiritual Light!

4. The purpose of life is spiritual transformation from a reactive being to a proactive being.

5. In the moment of our transformation, we make contact with the 99 percent realm.

6. Never—and that means never—lay blame on other people or external events.

7. Resisting our reactive impulses creates lasting Light.

8. Reactive behavior creates intense sparks of Light, but eventually leaves darkness in its wake.

9. Obstacles are our opportunity to connect to the Light.

10. The greater the obstacle, the greater the potential Light.

11. When challenges appear overwhelming, inject certainty. The Light is always there!

12. All of the negative traits that you spot in others are merely a reflection of your own negative traits. Only by fixing yourself can you change others.

And finally, ultimately:

Love thy neighbor as thyself. All the rest is mere commentary.

Now go and learn.

A Brief History of Kabbalah

Abraham
(c. 2000 BCE)

The first written work on Kabbalah, called The Book of Formation, was authored by Abraham the Patriarch, the father of Judaism, Christianity, and Islam, more than 4,000 years ago. The Book of Formation is said to contain all the mysteries of the universe, yet it is only a few pages long. How can that be?

Of course, a great deal can be shown in a concise way, as Einstein proved with his famous formula, $E=mc^2$. Within these five characters are mathematical insights that help define and explain the mysteries of time, space, energy, and matter.

The Book of Formation is another such formula. Just as Einstein's formula required extensive mathematical knowledge, only those who were adept in the mystical arts of Kabbalah were able to penetrate the secrets within this holy book.

The Seed of *All* Religion

This ancient Kabbalist text influenced most of the world's great religions. It is cited both in the Book of Mormon and the Koran as the Book of Abraham.

Important portions of Abraham's Kabbalistic wisdom were also given by the Patriarch to some of his children who were then sent to the East to develop the spiritual paths that we know of today, such as Zen Buddhism and Hinduism. In truth, all religious systems and spiritual doctrines can be traced back to Kabbalistic wisdom.

The *complete* body of Kabbalistic wisdom was handed down many generations later to the greatest prophet the world had ever seen.

Moses
(1446 BCE)

Over 3,300 years ago, Moses stood atop Mount Sinai and received two tablets inscribed with ten commandments. In truth, the story of Moses and the Ten Commandments is a code that has *nothing* to do with the literal meaning of the biblical verses.

Perhaps the most common misconception is the concept of Ten Commandments. God does not command. And God does not dictate. Nor does God punish and reward. If you stick your finger into a wall socket and electrocute yourself, it's illogical to say that electricity punished you. Likewise, if you plug in an air conditioner on a sweltering hot day to get some relief, we do not say the force of electricity rewarded you. Rather *how* you interact with this force determines whether there is pain or pleasure.

The term *Ten Commandments* is a code for the ten dimensions (see page 78) and the spiritual energy and Light that dwells in the 99 percent reality. If we plug into this Light through ego, it's a painful short-circuit. If we plug in proactively, the Light goes on.

An Ancient Technology

Moses utilized the technology of Kabbalah to plug our 1 percent world into the 99 percent. *That* is the meaning of the Ten

Commandments and the revelation story. Moses then encoded this Kabbalistic wisdom in the concealed language of metaphor and parable, writing it down in what became known as the Five Books of Moses, or the Bible. The true secrets, however, were hidden, and only passed onward by word of mouth to a few worthy descendants in each succeeding generation.

Moses failed to bring an end to the chaotic version of this game of life on Sinai because the Israelites were not yet prepared to sacrifice their egos. They complained and whined and griped about life in the desert and demanded that Moses return them to Pharaoh. As we learned in this book, these complaints, recorded in the Bible, are a code. *Egypt* is a code for the material world. *Pharaoh* represents the human ego.

The Israelites did not want to let go of their reactive egocentric behavior. This negative behavior then created an opening for the anti-Kabbalists, also known as the mix-multitude, to sabotage the revelation event of Sinai. These anti-Kabbalists instigated the building of the golden calf. This event disconnected the world from the 99 percent. The tablets and Moses' Kabbalistic wisdom were then concealed inside the Ark of the Covenant, destined to be hidden away for millennia.

Pythagoras
(c. 400 BCE)

Pythagoras was one of the greatest minds of history. Music, mathematics, and other sciences owe a great debt to this man. According to Hermippus of Smyrna (c. 200 BCE), the ancient biographer, Pythagoras took all of his ideas and theories from the doctrines of the Israelites and Moses. Hermippus even accuses Pythagoras of plagiarizing this Kabbalistic, biblical wisdom, using it as his own and then introducing it among the Greeks.

Dr. Seth Pancoast (1844–1916) was professor of microscopic anatomy and physiology at the Institutes of Medicine at Penn Medical University. He, along with Thomas Edison, was an original Fellow and founder of the Theosophical Society. Dr. Pancoast wrote:

> *Pythagoras was one of the most remarkable men of his day; not only was he learned in the ordinary sense beyond his time, but he was a Kabbalist of the highest order.*

Iamblichus (AD 250–325), the best-known ancient biographer of Pythagorus, wrote:

> *. . . Pythagoras conversed with the prophets who were the descendants of Moses the physiologist . . .*

Plato
(c. 400 BCE)

Isaac Newton, writing in his theological manuscripts, speculated that Plato borrowed secret knowledge from the Kabbalists and used it as the basis of his own philosophical system. Newton's teacher, Henry More, also said Plato's wisdom was taken from the Kabbalists. Corroborating Newton and More, Dr. Pancoast wrote,

"Plato too was an earnest and most intelligent Kabbalist."

While many great minds of history were given limited exposure to this wisdom, the time to reveal the *complete* Kabbalah in manuscript form would have to wait for the greatest Kabbalist of all.

Jesus
(Rabbi Joshua the son of Joseph, 1st Century)

According to Kabbalists, he was the potential messiah of his generation, known as the Messiah, son of Joseph. He learned the Kabbalistic technique of ritual immersion in water and Kabbalistic meditation from *Yochanan the Immerser* (John the Baptist). In the Gospels of Thomas, which contain Jesus' secret teachings given to only his closest disciples, he teaches that the Light is the origin of all humanity and that each person is a spark of the Divine. All people are considered, "children of the Light." It was Kabbalah that he used to perform acts of healing and other wonders.

Anti-Kabbalists reported his Kabbalistic practices to the Romans—just as they did all the other Kabbalists of this era—and he was executed.

The Other Persecuted Kabbalists

The great sage known as Akiva, was publicly skinned alive by the Roman Empire in front of some 20,000 spectators. The Kabbalist Ishmael, the son of Elisha, was flayed, his face torn from his head and given to the daughter of the Roman emperor. The sage known as Gamaliel was beheaded. All these sages were masters of Kabbalistic practice.

Both Jesus and Akiva encoded all of their Kabbalistic wisdom in a deceptively simple and profound verse taken from the Old Testament: *"Love thy neighbor as thyself"*.

The Zohar states that the death of a great Kabbalistic sage helps to purify and cleanse the sins of his or her generation. Consequently, Kabbalists understand that these great souls were also killed to cleanse the sins of their fellow Israelites, who still refused to surrender their *ego*, just as they refused on Mount Sinai.

These great Kabbalistic sages were considered to be "Sons of God." In fact, the Zohar says that *anyone* who studies its Kabbalistic wisdom is called "the Son of the Holy One" (Son of God) and "the Son of the Father." However, these and other Kabbalistic secrets were forcibly concealed from the masses for millennia.

Worse, with most of the Kabbalists now slaughtered, both Rome and the anti-Kabbalists were on the verge of eradicating Kabbalah *permanently* from the landscape of civilization. But Akiva left one student behind who was called upon by his master to keep the wisdom alive. His name was *Shimon, the Son of Yohai.*

Rabbi Shimon the son of Yohai
(2nd Century, c. AD 160)

He was ordained as a Kabbalistic master and teacher by the great Judah Ben Baba, who willingly sacrificed his own life in order to ordain the eminent Kabbalist Shimon.

Baba's action violated Roman law, and Judah's body was pummeled and sliced by more than 300 arrows and lances.

The giant of all Kabbalists, Shimon bar Yohai was sentenced to death by Roman emperor Hadrian after yet another anti-Kabbalist reported Shimon bar Yohai to Roman authorities.

But Rome was no match for this Kabbalist. He took this opportunity to embark on a historic spiritual quest by secluding himself in a cave in Meron, Israel, for the next 13 years of his life. Burying himself neck deep in the ground each day, he was able to climb great spiritual heights through Kabbalistic meditation. His 13-year seclusion merited him the task of revealing the *complete* body of knowledge on Kabbalah called the Zohar.

The Zohar was and continues to be the greatest work of Kabbalah.

Sorcery or Science

Throughout history, anti-Kabbalists feared the Zohar because of its power and the truths it spoke. Others considered the Zohar manuscript a work on mysticism and magic. In hindsight, the reason is obvious:

The Zohar expounds upon ideas and concepts that were centuries ahead of their time.

In an age where science determined that the world was flat, The Zohar depicts our planet as spherical, with people experiencing day and night in different time zones.

The Zohar describes the moment of creation as a Big Bang–like explosion.

It speaks of a universe that exists in ten dimensions.

It explores the notion of parallel universes and black holes.

In ancient times, these speculations were heretical and frightening. Yet, they are not the most fantastic to appear in the Zohar. That designation belongs to the following idea . . .

Shimon bar Yohai says the Zohar is *more* than a book of secrets and wisdom. It is a powerful energy-giving instrument, a life-saving tool that, in and of itself, is imbued with the power to bring genuine peace, protection, healing, and fulfillment to those who *possess* the actual physical books.

There's more.

Like the monolith in the film 2001: *A Space Odyssey*, the Zohar can ignite the soul of a generation, sparking profound change and transformation within the consciousness of human beings and society. In other words, just as a light bulb illumines a darkened room revealing objects previously unseen, the Light of the Zohar enlightens the minds of humans to the hidden mysteries of the cosmos *simply by its presence*.

According to the Kabbalists, these unseen influences will eventually help shape the destiny of humankind as knowledge of the Zohar's teachings increases in our world.

The Dark Ages

The great Kabbalist Shimon bar Yohai stated that there would come a day when even a six-year-old child would be able to delve into the spiritual wisdom of Kabbalah. But until that time arrived, the original manuscripts of the Zohar had to remain concealed. They were then hidden away for centuries. The dimming of the Zohar's spiritual Light coincides with the Dark Ages, a time when every aspect of civilization, including education, science, and communication, was almost totally dormant.

Kabbalist Moses Deleon
(13th Century, c. 1270)

The great Spanish Kabbalist Moses Deleon of Toledo, Spain, made a startling discovery when he came upon the Zohar manuscripts in the 13th century. In fact, the recent discovery of the Dead Sea Scrolls pales in comparison to the finding of the Zohar.

The Zohar itself, and the Book of Daniel, both state that its concealment would last 1,200 years (100 years for each of the 12 tribes of Israel), beginning from the time of the destruction of the Holy Temple.

The Temple in Jerusalem was destroyed by Romans in the year 70 BCE

Moses Deleon revealed the Zohar in the year 1270—1,200 years later, as the Zohar and the Book of Daniel had anticipated.

The Monolith Effect

Moses Deleon's discovery generally went unnoticed by the world. But it marked a historically significant turning point as the Light of the Zohar radiated into the world for the first time in human history. Its mystical verses rendered the work inaccessible to the masses; however, Kabbalists assert that the energy emanating from its mystical text sparked the collective unconscious of a generation.

Some five years after Deleon published the Zohar, famed philosopher Roger Bacon foresaw a future where ships would travel underwater, machines would fly in the sky, and boats would voyage without sails or oars. It sounded a lot like mysticism to the people who dwelt in his generation, and Bacon was soon imprisoned for heresy.

Not long after, Nicholas Oresme, philosopher, economist, mathematician, physicist, and one of the principal founders of modern science, taught about the motion of the earth, 200 years before Copernicus. He wrote about the nature, reflection, and speed of light—concepts explored at great length by the Zohar.

The Authentic Holy Grail

The search for the long lost Holy Grail has been documented in contemporary books and movies, as well as in stories and poems dating from medieval times. The Grail has been variously identified as a cup of salvation, a stone, a blood-red sword, and even as a path of spiritual transformation. Common symbols appearing in Grail legends include knights, a rose, a Tree of Life, and the Grail castle. But here's what's most interesting: All of these descriptions and symbols, down to the smallest detail, are found in the Zohar.

What's more, the most famous Holy Grail author, Wolfram Von Eschenbach, said he received his Grail story from a Jewish mystic in Toledo, Spain, in the 13th century. The Zohar first appeared in Toledo, Spain, in the 13th century—a time when Kabbalah was the best known and most sought-after form of spiritual wisdom in Spain. The Kabbalists of France, specifically one known as Isaac the Blind, wrote a letter warning the Spanish Kabbalists against revealing these Kabbalistic secrets in public, for they were being peddled and circulated out in the marketplace.

According to the Catholic Encyclopedia, the most detailed account of the Grail's true nature is found in a 13th century book entitled *The Grand St. Graal*. In this medieval manuscript, the Holy

Grail is called "a book of astonishing Light." Furthermore, simply gazing at the Grail is said to banish death and impart healing. The Zohar's true identity as the elusive Holy Grail will be more fully explored in a future book.

Kabbalist Isaac Luria (the Ari)
(16th Century, 1534–1572)

Kabbalist Isaac Luria was a child prodigy who delved deeply into the mystical wonders of the Zohar. Nicknamed "the Ari," or the Holy Lion, he produced a historic commentary on the Zohar that removed many of its layers of complexity. The Ari's teachings became the definitive school of Kabbalistic thought. Christian scholars soon translated his writings into Latin, allowing the Ari's Kabbalistic wisdom to influence the greatest minds of the Renaissance, which, in turn, helped ignite the scientific revolution of the next century. All the material in this book is rooted in Lurianic Kabbalah.

Opening the Vaults

Also in the 16th century, the Kabbalist Abraham Azulai (1570–1643) issued a decree that removed any and all prohibitions concerning the learning of Kabbalah, retroactive from the year 1540. This would be the first time in human history that Kabbalah could be made available to everyone, even a six-year-old child.

Agent 007

On a lighter note, British secret agent James Bond owes part of his existence to Kabbalah.

Dr. John Dee (1527–1608) was England's leading mathematician and scientist. Scholar Dr. Matt Goldish calls John Dee the most brilliant man of his age. Internationally famous for his genius, Dee contributed to science, mathematics, philosophy, geography, architecture, and art. He was also the official Royal Astrologer advising Queen Elizabeth I. According to professor and scholar Deborah Harkness of the University of California, Davis, Dee was also a mystic of Kabbalah:

> John Dee was probably the most important and influen-
> tial natural philosopher and scientist, living and working in
> England in the 16th century. John Dee was enormously
> influenced by Kabbalah. He had an extensive Kabbalistic
> library. The best one in England hands down in the 16th
> century. It was Kabbalah that drove all of his work.

According to Harkness, Dee was convinced that Kabbalah could reveal the hidden truth about the natural world through hidden messages that God embedded into this physical reality.

Donald McCormick, a foreign editor at the *London Sunday Times* and author of *A History of the British Secret Service*, was an acquaintance of Ian Fleming, creator of James Bond. In his book, McCormick says that Fleming learned that the Kabbalist Dee had done some espionage work on behalf of the queen. He had advised the British secret service on coding and cryptology techniques. Dee signed his private dispatches to the queen with two circles (00), indicating that he was the "eyes" of the Queen, and the number seven (7), an important Kabbalistic number.

Fleming based James Bond upon John Dee, using the mystic's signature 007 as the insignia for his British secret agent.

Kabbalah and the Scientific Revolution
(17th Century)

The 17th century experienced an abrupt and *unexplainable* explosion of scientific advancement. Scholars and scientists had no idea why this sudden scientific outburst took place. On the basis of new evidence, however, some scholars now argue that it was Kabbalah that profoundly influenced the greatest scientists and mathematicians of the 17th century. This was a time a lot of different than our own. In our day, science and spirituality wage war on one another. During the 17th century, the lines between spirituality and science, physics and metaphysics, were virtually nonexistent.

An Eruption of Knowledge

The great historian Max Dimont writes in his best-selling book, *Jews, God, and History*, "Western philosophy and science, which had died with the Greeks and Romans in the second century AD, was reborn in the sixteenth and seventeenth centuries."

Dimont adds: "Something must have sparked this rebirth, but what?" Dimont credits Kabbalah: "This body of Kabalistic [sic] work may even have had a large share in the sudden efflorescence of science in the seventeenth century."

Concerning this sudden scientific revolution, scholar A. C. Crombie states in his book, *Medieval and Early Modern Science,* "Why such a revolution in methods of thought should have taken place is obscure."

But Dimont says examining the role of the medieval Kabbalists as scientists "may throw some light on the sudden eruption of scientific genius in Western Europe in the seventeenth century."

The Original Secret Wisdom

Professor Allison P. Coudert contends in her book, *The Impact of the Kabbalah in the 17th Century,* that "Lurianic Kabbalah deserves a place it has never received in the histories of western scientific and cultural developments."

For instance, the great mathematician Leibniz, who concurrently with Sir Isaac Newton invented calculus, resulting in those tiresome math classes we endured in high school, was profoundly influenced by Kabbalah.

Both Leibniz and Newton and their esteemed peers believed that Kabbalah personified an ancient secret wisdom, called *prisca theologia.* Prisca theologia refers to secret wisdom that God had covertly revealed to Moses on Mount Sinai. Leibniz, Newton, and the top scientists of the Renaissance believed that if this pure wisdom was rediscovered and revealed to the world in its genuine, uncorrupted form, it would bring about world peace. This secret wisdom would establish a foundation for a true universal religion, thereby eradicating the religious conflicts that have left the landscape of human civilization soaked in blood.

Coudert writes, "Kabbalistic writings were generally thought to be the most important single source for the recovery of this ancient wisdom . . . they represented the first and purest source of that divine knowledge."

In fact, Leibniz, one of the supreme intellects of the 17th century, told Swedish scholar Erik Benzelius about "his plans for a learned society which would combine Kabbalah, Calculus, mysticism, and mechanics."

The Two Isaacs: Luria and Newton

Sir Isaac Newton, the man most responsible for the scientific revolution and the launching of the Age of Enlightenment, was a serious student of Kabbalah. He event went so far as to learn the Hebrew language.

In his book, *The Religion of Isaac Newton*, scholar Frank Manuel says, "Moses knew the whole of the scientific truth—of this Newton was certain."

Scholar Richard Popkin says that Newton saw the Bible as "a cryptogram" that concealed the true secrets of the universe. Newton's view of the Bible was identical to the Kabbalists'.

Scholar George Zollschan, in his paper, "God's Sensorium: Newton's Kabbalistic Slip," states that Newton's famous description of space as *sensorium dei* is the result of Kabbalistic influence.

Sensorium dei means God causes creation and movement by "perceiving" rather than willing or speaking. This notion, Zollschan asserts, has only one precedent: the Kabbalistic teachings of the Ari (Isaac Luria).

It turns out that Newton owned his own personal copy of *Kabbalah Denudata*, the Latin translation of the Zohar and the Ari's Kabbalistic writings. Remarkably, some of Newton's

Dr. Pancoast wrote, "Newton was led to the discovery of these forces (law of attraction and repulsion) by his studies of the Kabbalah."

Scholar Serge Hutin even identified Newton as a "Christian Kabbalist."

Early 20th Century

It was not until the start of the 20th century that Kabbalist Rav Yehuda Ashlag, the most prolific mystic of the period, deciphered the writings of the Ari and the texts of the Zohar. It was a monumental and historic accomplishment. And now the wisdom of Kabbalah was more accessible than ever before. One did not need the brain power of a Newton or Plato to understand these awesome secrets. This, by the way, did not please certain factions in the religious community. In one of many cruel incidents by the anti-Kabbalists of his generation, Rav Ashlag was left lying in a pool of his own blood on the steps of his Learning Centre.

Undaunted, Rav Ashlag delved even deeper into the Zohar with devout fervor and unraveled its greatest secrets. But the vast majority of the world paid little attention to his historic action, nor could they perceive its influence.

Concepts such as relativity, space travel, healing, parallel universes, the origins of heart disease and its relationship to cholesterol, and matters affecting the welfare of humankind were encoded into the Zohar some 2,000 years ago. Rav Ashlag's genius lay in his ability to extrapolate these secrets from Kabbalistic texts.

The Zohar was now even more accessible and *out there* than it had been during the scientific revolution. It was *definitely* not a coincidence that the Zohar appeared in our secular world in the same century that saw more technological advancements than *all other centuries combined.*

Mid 20th Century

Rav Ashlag's chief disciple, Kabbalist Yehudah Brandwein, completed and published his master's monumental Zohar writings. Though pious and orthodox, Rav Brandwein was a man of the common people. He was especially loved by the so-called *nonreligious* types, which was an intriguing paradox. He was a gentle, unassuming, humble soul who scaled scaffolding on construction sites by day and then scaled lofty spiritual worlds by moonlight.

Rav Brandwein embraced everyone he met with unconditional love and acceptance, regardless of their religious observances or absence of them. He evoked a deep love in all those with whom he came in contact. Both atheists and devout believers had great reverence for him. Rav Brandwein left this world in 1969, after having passed the sacred torch to his beloved student, Kabbalist Rav Berg.

The Present Day

Rav Berg and his wife, Karen Berg, broke with 2,000 years of tradition and religious dogma and brought the wisdom of Kabbalah within the reach of everyone who had a sincere desire to learn. This daring act was not without cost. Like most of the Kabbalists throughout history, they endured physical violence, extreme verbal abuse, and emotional pain and suffering at the hands of anti-Kabbalists—those who were determined to keep the Kabbalah from regular people who sought answers from religion that went beyond the traditional response, "Because it is written."

Corruption

The Zohar *itself* warned that the "governing religious authority" would always try to prevent people from claiming the spiritual power that was rightly theirs. Their objective was to act as the intermediary between humankind and the Divine—to operate a tollbooth that stood between God and our soul. Religious authorities would fear the universal wisdom of Kabbalah because it empowers individuals (not rabbis and priests) with tools to connect *directly* to the infinite, boundless Light of Creation. That would mean their demise as gatekeepers to heaven.

Rav Berg's master, Rav Brandwein, had told him that because the spiritual wisdom of Kabbalah was jealously guarded throughout so much of history, 95 percent of people had turned their backs on religion (and you are probably one of them), for "religion" had failed (by design) to rid people of their personal problems, pain, and suffering. Harsh realities, but the truth, nevertheless.

Now that Rav Berg and Karen opened the ancient vaults of Kabbalah to the masses, people everywhere have an opportunity to understand why we exist; how we arrived here; and how we can remove pain, suffering, torment, fear, and chaos from our personal lives.

The secret is finally out, and that is why you are able to read this book.

More from National Best-Selling Author Yehuda Berg

The 72 Names of God: Technology for the Soul™

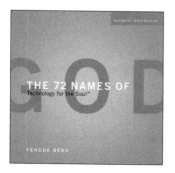

The story of Moses and the Red Sea is well known to almost everyone; it's even been an Academy Award–winning film. What is not known, according to the internationally prominent Kabbalist Rabbi Yehuda Berg, is that a state-of-the-art technology is encoded and concealed within that biblical story. This technology is called the 72 Names of God, and it is the key—your key—to ridding yourself of depression, stress, creative stagnation, anger, illness, and other physical and emotional problems. In fact, the 72 Names of God is the oldest, most powerful tool known to mankind—far more powerful than any 21st century high-tech know-how when it comes to eliminating the garbage in your life so that you can wake up and enjoy life each day. Indeed, the 72 Names of God is the ultimate pill for anything and everything that ails you because it strikes at the DNA level of your soul.

The power of the 72 Names of God operates strictly on a soul level, not a physical one. It's about spirituality, not religiosity. Rather than being limited by the differences that divide people, the wisdom of the Names transcends humanity's age-old quarrels and belief systems to deal with the one common bond that unifies all people and nations: the human soul.

Kabbalah: Red String

The Red String is the most widely recognized tool of The Kabbalah Centre. Rarely a week goes by without a feature article or a television program discussing the celebrities who wear it, calling it "the trend that doesn't end." The Red String is the best-selling kabbalistic product in the world.

Yehuda Berg, author of national best-seller *The 72 Names of God: Technology for the Soul*™, continues to attract the public's interest with his latest book, *Kabbalah: Red String*. In it, he reveals the antidote to the negative effects of the dreaded "Evil Eye."

Here he reveals the ancient methodology that fuels the wisdom of the Red String, and readers will learn why celebrities and millions of others aren't leaving home without it.

Dreams

In *Dreams*, national best-selling author Yehuda Berg lifts the curtain of reality to reveal secrets of dream interpretation that have remained hidden for centuries.

Readers will discover a millennia-old system for understanding dreams and will learn powerful techniques to help them find soul mates, discover career opportunities, be alerted to potential illness in the body, improve relationships with others, develop an overall deeper awareness, and much more.

The dream state is a mysterious and fascinating realm in which the rules of reality do not apply. This book is the key to navigating the dreamscape, where the answers to all of life's questions await.

More products that can help you bring the wisdom of Kabbalah into your life

Becoming Like God
By Michael Berg

At the age of 16, Kabbalistic scholar Michael Berg began the herculean task of translating the Zohar, Kabbalah's chief text, from its original Aramaic into its first complete English translation. The Zohar, which consists of 23 volumes, is considered a compendium of virtually all information pertaining to the universe, and its wisdom is only beginning to be verified today.

During the ten years he worked on the Zohar, Michael Berg discovered the long-lost secret for which mankind has searched for more than 5,000 years: how to achieve our ultimate destiny. *Becoming Like God* reveals the transformative method by which people can actually break free of what is called "ego nature" to achieve total joy and lasting life.

Berg puts forth the revolutionary idea that for the first time in history, an opportunity is being made available to humankind: an opportunity to Become Like God.

The Secret
By Michael Berg

Like a jewel that has been painstakingly cut and polished, *The Secret* reveals life's essence in its most concise and powerful form. Michael Berg begins by showing you how our everyday understanding of our purpose in the world is literally backwards.

Whenever there is pain in our lives—indeed, whenever there is anything less than complete joy and fulfillment—this basic misunderstanding is the reason.

The Essential Zohar
By Rav Berg

The Zohar has traditionally been known as the world's most esoteric and profound spiritual document, but Rav Berg has dedicated his life to making this wisdom universally available. The vast wisdom and Light of the Zohar came into being as a gift to all humanity, and *The Essential Zohar* at last explains this gift to the world.

Audio Resources

The Power of Kabbalah Tape Series

The Power of Kabbalah is nothing less than a user's guide to the universe. Move beyond where you are right now to where you truly want to be—emotionally, spiritually, and creatively. This exciting tape series brings you the ancient, authentic teaching of Kabbalah in a powerful, practical audio format.

Creating Miracles in Your Life

We're used to thinking of a miracle as something that happens at the whim of God. But the Kabbalists have long taught that the true power to create miracles is present in each and every one of us—if only we can learn to access that power and put it into practice. This inspiring tape series shows how to do exactly that. Order it now, and enter the zone of the miraculous!

The Zohar

Bringing the Zohar from near oblivion to wide accessibility has taken many decades. It is an achievement of which we are truly proud and grateful.
— Michael Berg

Composed more than 2,000 years ago, the Zohar is a set of 23 23books, a commentary on biblical and spiritual matters in the form of conversations among spiritual masters. But to describe the Zohar only in physical terms is greatly misleading. In truth, the Zohar is nothing less than a powerful tool for achieving the most important purposes of our lives. It was given to all humankind by the Creator to bring us protection, to connect us with the Creator's Light, and ultimately to fulfill our birthright of true spiritual transformation.

Eighty years ago, when the Kabbalah Centre was founded, the Zohar had virtually disappeared from the world. Few people in the general population had ever heard of it. Whoever sought to read it—in any country, in any language, at any price—faced a long and futile search.

Today all this has changed. Through the work of the Kabbalah Centre and the editorial efforts of Michael Berg, the Zohar is now being brought to the world, not only in the original Aramaic language but also in English.

The new English Zohar provides everything for connecting to this sacred text on all levels: the original Aramaic text for scanning; an English translation; and clear, concise commentary for study and learning.

The Kabbalah Centre
The International Leader in the Education of Kabbalah

Since its founding, the Kabbalah Centre has had a single mission: to improve and transform people's lives by bringing the power and wisdom of Kabbalah to all who wish to partake of it.

Through the lifelong efforts of Rav Berg, his wife Karen, and the great spiritual lineage of which they are a part, an astonishing 3.5 million people around the world have already been touched by the powerful teachings of Kabbalah. And each year, the numbers are growing!

As the leading source of Kabbalistic wisdom with 50 locations around the world, the Kabbalah Centre offers you a wealth of resources, including:

- The English Zohar, the first-ever comprehensive English translation of the foundation of Kabbalistic wisdom. In 23 beautifully bound volumes, this edition includes the full Aramaic text, the English translation, and detailed commentary, making this once-inaccessible text understandable to all.

- A full schedule of workshops, lectures, and evening classes for students at all levels of knowledge and experience.

- CDs, audiotapes and videotapes, and books in English and ten other languages.

- One of the Internet's most exciting and comprehensive websites, www.kabbalah.com—which receives more than

100,000 visitors each month.

- A constantly expanding list of events and publications to help you live *The Secret* and other teachings of Kabbalah with greater understanding and excitement.

Discover why the Kabbalah Centre is one of the world's fastest-growing spiritual organizations. Our sole purpose is to improve people's lives through the teachings of Kabbalah. Let us show you what Kabbalah can do for you!

Each Kabbalah Centre location hosts free introductory lectures. For more information on Kabbalah or on these and other products and services, call 1-800-KABBALAH.

Wherever you are, there's a Kabbalah Centre—because now you can call 1-800-KABBALAH from almost anywhere, 18 hours a day, and get answers or guidance right over the telephone. You'll be connected to distinguished senior faculty who are on hand to help you understand Kabbalah as deeply as you want to—whether it involves recommending a course of study; deciding which books/tapes to take or in which order to take them; discussing the material; or anything else you wish to know about Kabbalah.

Book Clubs

If you want more information on *The Power of Kabbalah* and would like to share your ideas and experiences with others, take advantage of *The Power of Kabbalah* book clubs, located throughout the world. Or to start your own, call 1-877-KCLASSES or visit our website at www.powerofkabbalah.com.

CALL 1-800-KABBALAH for a FREE ten-minute personal consultation with a highly trained Power of Kabbalah teacher. Find out exactly how the Power of Kabbalah can help you with the issues you are facing in your life right now!

For my daughters,
Honour and **Ava**,

may they rise to their potential
and use their gifts to bring
Light forever to their world and
to the rest of the universe.